global style

global style

LESLEY DILCOCK

photography CATHERINE GRATWICKE
text contributor JO LEEVERS

RYLAND
PETERS
& SMALL

For Letty

Designer Megan Smith
Senior editor Annabel Morgan
Location research manager Kate Brunt
Location researcher Sarah Hepworth
Production Patricia Harrington
Art director Gabriella Le Grazie
Publishing director Anne Ryland

Stylist Lesley Dilcock
Text contributor Jo Leevers

First published in the United States in 2000
by Ryland Peters & Small
Cavendish House
51–55 Mortimer Street
London W1N 7TD
10 9 8 7 6 5 4 3 2 1

Printed and bound in China by
Toppan Printing Co.

ISBN 1-84172-049-6

A CIP catalog record for this book is available
from the Library of Congress

CONTENTS

INTRODUCTION 6

1 INSPIRATIONS 8
  Color 12
  Surface + texture 20
  Textiles 26

2 ELEMENTS 34
  Furniture 38
  Lamps + lighting 48
  Kitchenware + tableware 52
  Collections 64

3 ROOMS 78
  Living spaces 82
  Kitchens + eating areas 94
  Bedrooms 104
  Bathrooms 114
  Workspaces 120
  Gardens + garden rooms 128

STOCKISTS + SUPPLIERS 138
PICTURE CREDITS 140
INDEX 142
ACKNOWLEDGMENTS 144

introduction

Global style is first and foremost about a relaxed approach to interiors. The look stems from a passion for the unusual and the eclectic. It combines the ordinary and the unique, the everyday and the idiosyncratic—Mexican glassware paired with vintage Japanese silks, an African stool beside a high-tech stainless-steel refrigerator. In a world that is shrinking, it celebrates difference and individuality, and rejects the uniform and homogeneous. And, best of all, it is endlessly flexible—whether you are a pared-down minimalist or a magpie who loves clutter, global style will be at home in your home.

The inspiration to bring global style into your home may be a treasured find from a trip overseas or something less tangible—a picture in a magazine of the jewel colors of an Indian palace or a film that shows the desert at sunrise. Whatever your inspiration, the aim is not to create themed rooms or display artefacts in a way that shouts "look where I've been." Instead, it is a low-key approach, where global objects are integrated seamlessly with your existing space and possessions to create rooms that are interesting, beautiful and, above all, lived in.

One of the main attractions of global pieces is that they are often handcrafted, giving them an appeal that flat-packed goods from the local mall cannot match. Life is not easy for people in a developing country, but often they hold fast to tradition in the face of adversity. When buying, ask about fair trade or, if abroad, buy direct from cooperative groups or the maker. Some countries impose export restrictions for older items, but going global is not really about collecting priceless antiques. Instead, it celebrates the modern and everyday, focusing on items that amuse, intrigue, and please the eye.

GLOBAL STYLE *To fall in love with an object, color, or texture and want to see it in your home has no boundaries of cost or country—it's entirely personal. Oriental ceramics (opposite), salvaged items (above left), ceremonial pieces (above center and above far right), or handcrafted souvenirs (above right) will all bring you huge amounts of pleasure.*

COLOR/ SURFACE + TEXTURE/ TEXTILES

inspirations

COLORS, TEXTURES, SURFACES, AND TEXTILES HAVE ALWAYS PROVED A

Since the earliest times, voyagers have returned from distant lands inspired by all they have seen and experienced on their travels, bringing with them the exotic and unusual to display in their homes. Colors, textures, surfaces, and textiles have always proved a particularly rich source of inspiration, for they are at the very heart of a country's character, inextricably linked to its customs and history. In a contemporary home, different influences from around the world can provide the basis for a truly individual and stylish interior. The slippery sheen of Chinese silk, the powdery surface of a sun-baked mud wall, or the feeling of cool Latin American tiles underfoot—all these sights and sensations can provide the inspiration for a uniquely exotic global home.

PARTICULARLY RICH SOURCE OF INSPIRATION

Among the most immediate sources of inspiration are the color palettes associated with different countries and cultures, from the vivid, arresting hues of India and Mexico, to the mellow, earthy shades of Africa and the calming, neutral tones of Asia. Textures and surfaces are just as memorable— the crumbly texture of a whitewashed wall, the scratched surface of a beaten copper bowl, or the knobbly ridges of a Japanese *tatami* mat can all stick in the memory.

Further inspiration may come from textiles and fabrics, which bring a rich reminder of a country's traditions into a room. Techniques and designs are still handed down from parent to child, often in the face of great hardship or the increasingly pervasive lure of MTV culture.

A bold and uninhibited use of color is a fundamental characteristic of global style. From attention-grabbing brights to dark, earthy hues, the inhabitants of exotic and distant countries are not afraid to embrace color and all it stands for. Under their intensely lit skies, there is no reticence, no shying away from those shades that leap out, clash, or clamor for attention. Color is fully exploited for what it is best at doing: bringing an infusion of much-needed vibrancy and cheer.

color

COLOR + DEPTH *Experiment with richly contrasting hues (opposite) clashing saturated colors (left) or a harmony of tones in the same color, but in varying shades (above). A personal kaleidescope of colors is the aim.*

VIBRANT COLOR

BOLD + BRIGHT *India favors the most exciting of jeweled brights. This flamboyant pink tie-dyed silk (below) is produced by pinching and knotting tiny areas of cloth and carries the* bandhani *motif of a simple dot. Dazzling Mexican striped wool ponchos and blankets blend harmoniously with similarly exuberant Indian textiles (right). The strikingly colored embroideries studded with tiny mirrors are created by Gujerati and Rajasthani tribes. For a stunning centerpiece, try alternatives to the usual fruit bowl. This South African wire bowl (left), decorated with beads and washers, is set aglow with the addition of ripe oranges.*

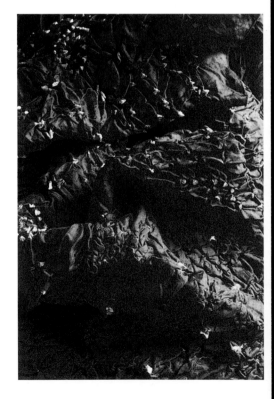

In hot tropical climates, intense, vibrant colors are needed to stand up to glaring sun and dark shade. India thrives on color, from the hot pinks of women's saris to the luminous chalky blue that high-ranking Brahmin use to paint their houses in Jaipur. Color is used purely to please the eye but also has a deeper significance: red, for example, represents passion and joy, and Indian women often marry in red saris. In Gujarat, *toran* cloths embroidered in crimson and pink and embellished with mirrorwork are hung above doorways to bring good luck. The clear, strong colors brighten harsh landscapes and hard lives.

Red is the predominant shade of China, found everywhere from commercial calligraphy to temple banners. The most popular bright red represents joy and luck, but red is such a significant color that there is a huge variety of phrases used to describe its shades, such as coral, fresh red, and sacrificial red. In modern homes, orange or red brings warmth and depth to a room. Alternatively, touches of red work well as a dramatic highlight in an understated scheme.

To the Chinese, green represents harmony, and it is also the color of the tropics, found in the vibrant green of rice paddies and glossy palm fronds. Rich deep yellow is another vivid shade seen all over India and Asia Pacific. Marigold blooms are laid as offerings in Indian temples, while wandering *saddhus,* or holy men, are clad in saffron robes. In Thailand, novice Buddhist monks wear robes of a similar shade. Rich saffron or gold creates a bold backdrop for a room and brings a meditative, templelike calm.

Indigo blue, extracted from the leaves of the indigo plant, has long been the cheapest source of blue dye the world over. In a contemporary home, deep ultramarine will establish a serene, reflective atmosphere, while the bold, zingy cobalt shade that Mexicans call *azul anul* works well in kitchens and bathrooms, and clear turquoise and aquamarine are the soothing shade of warm tropical seas.

EARTHY COLOR

Earth tones are just what their name suggests—pigments derived from the earth. Natural mineral and vegetable ingredients produce colors like deep brown, dun, rusty red, copper green, and sandstone yellow—rich, subtle hues that are reassuringly honest and elemental.

In Africa, earth tones predominate in architecture, textiles, and pottery. Iron-rich red clay is used to make mud huts that blend almost seamlessly into the landscape. In some areas, walls are decorated by pressing maize cobs into the drying mud to create abstract patterns. Geometric shapes and flowers are also painted onto houses in earthy shades—ocher and red from clay, white from chalk or limestone, and black from soot.

Red, ocher, and white glazes or slips are also painted on to African pottery, while other earth tones come from unglazed coil pots fired in open-air kilns, so that black scorch marks mingle with the earthy red of the clay. Earth tones are also found in woven raffia cloths that are dyed with natural pigments and in the dense, dark wood used for furniture and bowls.

A paler tone comes from the crumbly mud called *pisé* that is used to build homes on the edge of the Moroccan Sahara. It dries to a warm, honey shade that can be recreated in the modern home with hard-wearing concrete or stone. Other mellow, earthy tones come from bare wood and natural matting, both of which can be used alongside darker shades to provide contrast within a restrained palette. In Asia, coconut fibers are used to make warm brown matting, while seagrass retains its natural beige hue since it is impermeable to dye.

At the darkest end of the spectrum is the lustrous sheen of handmade black pottery. This is made in Africa, India, and the Americas by refiring pots in a dry grass fire or closed kiln that starves the clay of oxygen. Buffing the finished pot produces a deep, metallic luster.

EARTH TONES *Harmonious tones from the different continents of the world can be integrated quite happily (opposite left and right). A Kuba cloth from Zaire (left) forms a backdrop to a shelf that holds Indian copper bowls and an African basket. Natural fibers play a large part in the earthy color palette. This banana-fibre notebook (below) is scattered with modern Kenyan metal paper clips, made especially for the tourist trade, but charming and evocative nonetheless.*

NEUTRAL COLOR

NATURAL HUES *A palette of neutrals may sound uninspiring, but the global home can bring far more interest to this color scheme than the magnolia walls it suggests. The beauty of shape and form can be greatly appreciated, as in the subtle modeling of this head of Buddha displayed in a tranquil bathroom (right), while pale tones allow the contrasting texture and finish of different objects to be admired (opposite and below).*

Neutrals—cream, white, beige, and brown—bring a relaxed, calming atmosphere to a room. The neutral palette is typically oriental, and Japanese interiors have long relied on the power of pale walls, natural wood, and opaque paper screens to convey a sense of tranquility and repose.

All over the world, white represents purity and simplicity. To prevent it from feeling too stark or clinical, combine it with interesting textures. Mix crushed shells, tiny gray or white pebbles, or hemp fibers into white plaster and leave roughly plastered walls unpainted. All-white interiors are the perfect backdrop for a dramatic infusion of exotic color and provide an ideal setting for richly colored textiles and dark wood pieces.

In Asia, bamboo is used to make everything from tablemats to building materials. Like wood, it mellows with age, giving a range of natural browns and yellows. For soft furnishings, unbleached canvas adds further texture, while gauze or voile curtains will keep the mood light, restful, and airy. Bleached or pickled floorboards can complement pale walls or, to stop a room from looking chilly, add warm jute or sisal underfoot or an oriental rug or kilim for an instant injection of comfort and warmth.

The urge to decorate one's home is a universal human instinct, whether that home is a hut or a palace. Color may be the most obvious and dramatic embellishment, but textural contrasts will also delight and intrigue the eye and are guaranteed to enliven any interior. Going global offers an alternative to minimalism and the sterility of the perfect finish. Instead, global style celebrates the natural finishes and handcrafted appeal of so many homes around the world and aims to capture something of their charm and individuality.

surface + texture

SURFACE + TEXTURE *Not for those who pride themselves on the immaculate finish of the paintwork, the polish on the silver, or the wall-to-wall carpets, but nevertheless the patina of age plays a big part in the character of a global home and has an appeal all of its own.*

DECORATIVE TILES *The designer owner of this home in Belgium has a passion for tiles. In the library (right), the marble fireplace was replaced with her own magnificent tiled creation—a melange of old and new, resplendent with Arabic calligraphy and antique finds. This collage idea would work well in any area of the home. The shower (opposite, left) brings a smile, as koi carp are nearly washed down the drain when the water flows. In the courtyard (opposite, right), a stellar theme creates a magical mood. In a Paris home (below), octagonal tiles form a pathway in a colored concrete floor.*

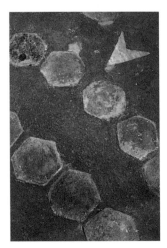

Textures and surfaces spotted on trips to exotic lands can provide a basis for a modern global interior. Imaginative combinations of contrasting surfaces and materials—a galvanized tin bucket on bleached floorboards, smooth shells and dry seed pods jumbled together in an old basket, woven matting on a rough-hewn stone floor—offer exciting variations of texture and shade.

Cool underfoot and easy to keep clean, tiles are a practical and versatile surface, and Middle Eastern craftsmen have long created them in dazzling shades to adorn their palaces and mosques. Tiles were an ancient Mesopotamian wall decoration revived by Islamic potters in the 9th century. European tiles took on new hues in the 15th century, when traders brought cargoes of china glazed in cobalt, turquoise, and purple from the East. These blue glazes influenced Iznik ceramics in Turkey, Spanish *azulejo*, Italian majolica, and Mexican tiles. Meanwhile, Islamic countries developed highly stylized floral and geometric motifs, while plain blue tiling in mosques is thought by some to symbolize a bridge between earthly worshippers and the heavens. Morocco is still a thriving center of *zillij,* or tilemaking, and contemporary designs will add originality to a modern bathroom or kitchen.

In the Thar desert of India, whole fortressed towns are built from sandstone. Some walls are whitewashed, but others retain their natural porous finish and amber glow. Flagstones or terracotta tiles will create a similarly warm and mellow effect in the contemporary home, while the uneven surface and pinkish hue of unpainted plaster walls echoes that of rough stone or *pisé* mud. To add interest to

TEXTURAL CONTRASTS WILL DELIGHT AND INTRIGUE THE EYE AND ENLIVEN ANY INTERIOR

WALLS + FLOORS *Breaking away from traditional surfaces is part of the informal aspect of the global home (opposite page). A painted concrete floor, unevenly plastered walls, flat and gloss paintwork, natural fiber matting for seating and flooring, and inlaid wooden ovals held in resin will all bring a global flavor to any home. The design of this hip New York advertising agency (right) was inspired by its former incarnation as a Chinese sweatshop. Red steel lockers divide different areas and are decorated with Chinese ideograms saying "friendship." The flooring is Chinese newspaper sealed with polyurethane varnish.*

uniformly smooth modern walls, mix a small amount of sand into latex paint to create a roughened and slightly more interesting texture.

Whitewashed or distempered walls possess an appealing chalky finish. Distemper was originally made from chalk mixed with water and animal size, but the finish rubbed off easily if the size was of poor quality. Paint stores now sell modern formulations that produce the same warm, creamy shade, but with improved binding power. Concrete, a common building material in many hot climates, is another cheap and durable medium for floors and walls, and can be given a global twist with the addition of a rich tint of color. And when polished or waxed, concrete develops a mellow tone reminiscent of natural stone.

Natural floorcoverings are another means of introducing texture into the modern home. In Asia, mats are used for sitting, eating, and sleeping on rather than walking on, and accordingly they tend to be less durable. Indian coir mats, made from woven coconut fibers, are more hardwearing and are ideal for busy areas. Jute is kind to bare feet, while sisal is long-lasting and versatile, and can be dyed in subtle shades. Japanese *tatami* mats are another natural flooring option. In Japan, realtors describe rooms as "two or three *tatami* mats" to convey their dimensions, as the mats come in a standard size.

FLAMBOYANT FABRICS *Global textiles will enrich any home. A London-based jewelry designer has used African fabrics to make slipcovers for traditional furniture to stunning effect (below right). Imagine these flamboyant Indian and African fabrics (opposite and below left) used in a similar way—sensational!*

textiles

Even in this age of mass production, textiles are still laboriously dyed, woven, sewn, and embroidered by hand in many countries all around the globe. Age-old designs and techniques are handed down from generation to generation, preserving traditional motifs and patterns. Proudly displayed or, even better, put to practical use in a contemporary bedroom or living room, colorful and exotic textiles bring the spirit of another culture into the heart of the modern home. Alternatively, finding a new use for global textiles—using a kilim as a wall hanging or an Indian sari as a curtain—is another way to integrate them into a contemporary interior.

PLAYING WITH PATTERN *Bold combinations of vividly colored and intricately designed textiles will enliven any room. A Turkish kilim has migrated from floor to wall, where it interplays with jewel-hued designer pillows (below). Kitchen chairs go global when decorated with multi-colored, multicultural textiles. Appliquéd and shell-trimmed Indian fabrics are used as chair covers; kilim seat covers and fabulous Victorian patchwork pillows are added to the eclectic mix (right and opposite).*

Indian textiles mean vibrant colors, from bright pink and yellow to the deep red and green found in embroidery from Rajasthan and Gujerat. Embroidered and appliquéd cloth, known as *katab* (from the English "cut up"), was once an important part of a Gujerati girl's dowry, and, although dowries are no longer legal, decorative cloths are still given when a bride enters her new home. These include wall hangings and bedspreads with bright, glittering mirrorwork and embroidery covering every inch.

The vivid, brilliant colors of Indian cloth are due to the fact that India discovered the secret of mordants long before Europe. These substances, which make vegetable dyes fast, included rusted iron, lime, vinegar, and even urine. Until the advent of aniline dyes in the mid-19th century, India's colorful cloths were highly prized. Today, the country's textiles hold fresh appeal, and there are cooperatives to buy from to make sure workers are paid a fair price. Indian textiles bring color and interest to the modern home: hang *torans* over doorways or on walls, swag silks and embroidery at windows, or use a richly colored sari as an exotic runner at a dining table.

Some hand-woven textiles are decorated with beads, coins, or shells, stemming from a time when beads and shells were forms of currency, and so symbolized wealth. Beaded cloths add magnificence to a room and should be displayed where there is space to appreciate them—a well-lit expanse of wall or deep stairway is ideal.

PRINTED, WOVEN, + EMBROIDERED

THE FABRIC OF SOCIETIES *This wealth of textiles from all over the globe will appeal to a wide range of tastes. Strong geometrics and colorful stripes are found in the rugs and wall hangings of North Africa and Turkey (top row, left and center) while tribal Kente cloth (top row, right) makes the liveliest of patchworks. In contrast, more delicate, intricate patterns can be found on antique kimonos (bottom row, left), the vibrant florals of modern Chinese silks (bottom row, center), and Moroccan tracery embroidered on cotton bedding (bottom row, right). Bolts of jewel-colored batik complete with the maker's label make a versatile and much coveted gift from an exotic vacation (opposite).*

Since the days of the legendary Silk Route, Oriental silk has been a much-coveted textile. In Japan, silk kimonos are reserved for important occasions, and are unpicked, cleaned, and re-sewn after each wearing. In the West, their rich colors, elaborate designs, and sumptuous fabrics makes them perfect decorative objects

Modern African textiles embrace the old and new: in Nigeria, modern weaves sparkle with lurex, but age-old mud cloth is still painstakingly produced in Mali. The Kuba people of Zaire make a raffia cloth that is woven by the men and embroidered with decorative motifs by the women. Kuba cloth is worn at ceremonies like funerals, where it is donned not only by family and friends, but is also used to dress the corpse. The earthy shades of such fabrics add a bold note to a neutral scheme and work well with wooden furniture and stripped floorboards. For an injection of color, look to the rich gold and electric blue of Kente cloth, made by the Ashanti people of Ghana.

In Indonesia, colorful, eye-dazzling designs are created by batik, in which wax is applied to cotton or silk before dying to stop the color from taking so that a fine pattern is built up. On the island of Java, women still hand-draw batik designs, but machine-printed imitations are fast encroaching upon this age-old skill. Batik makes attractive wallhangings or bedspreads, while cheaper sarongs make versatile throws or beach towels.

A rug is a focal point of any room, adding warmth and color. Flat woven rugs, best known by the Turkish word kilim, have a less formal feel than carpets and work well in modern rooms. Muslims are not allowed to represent human or animal forms for fear of idolatry, so carpets from Islamic countries are decorated with highly stylized motifs. The Moroccan version of the kilim, the *hanbel*, is traditionally used inside Berber tents to cover walls and floors. Kilims and woven saddlebags are hardwearing but flexible, so they can be used as upholstery fabrics.

CLOTHING *Some clothes are far too exciting to live in a closet or drawer. A fashion designer hangs inexpensive Indian silks around her dressing-room walls for a bright reminder of magical travels (opposite). More works of art than clothing, these children's dresses from Afghanistan are formally displayed to show the intricate mix of shells, beads, coins, and assorted other decorations that adorn them (above). In this Brussels apartment (right), a workroom is set aside for the owner to store her eclectic collection of fabrics and to run up outfits in anything from exotic batiks to Liberty prints.*

elements

ECLECTICISM AND ORIGINALITY ARE THE KEY WORDS—ELEMENTS FROM VERY

The elements of global style are furnishings, objects, and household items from all over the world. Choose interesting and expressive pieces to bring a global spin to a contemporary home. Be bold—mix old with new, cheap with expensive—think African baskets with Chinese silks, India metalware with Mexican glasses. Color and shape are important—the actual provenance of an article doesn't matter, as long as it interests and pleases the eye. If you are lucky enough to travel to exotic lands, look out for unusual and beautiful objects to bring back home. If you are unable to venture to distant countries, searching closer to home can be just as fruitful—there are countless hunting grounds for exotic items—specialized retailers, secondhand stores, even thrift shops.

DIFFERENT PLACES AND ERAS CAN COMBINE TO CREATE THE GLOBAL LOOK

Eclecticism and originality are two key words—pieces of furniture from very different places and eras can come together happily to create an entirely individual global look. One or two pieces can act as the focal point of a more understated room, while an exuberant collection of objects from north and south, east and west will bring vitality and personality to any home.

Using everyday household items such as kitchenware and tableware from exotic countries is a fun and inexpensive way to introduce global elements into the modern home. Buying ordinary, day-to-day objects is also something that can be done with a clear conscience—it brings home the spirit of a country without removing anything that may be a part of that country's cultural heritage.

Homes in exotic countries are often more sparsely and simply furnished than their western counterparts. Pride of place might go to a treasured marital bed that has been handed down through several generations, an ornately carved armoire or a child's crib. In the modern home, a few chosen items from a distant land can make a stronger statement than an abundance of furniture and ornaments. Simplicity is refreshing, and means that favorite items of furniture are given room to breathe, rather than having to compete for attention.

furniture

SIMPLE PIECES *The occasional table can come from interesting global backgrounds. This Indian ironing board (above and left) now sits in a London house. A modern Moroccan-inspired table (opposite) has a naive rawness that says global.*

CHAIRS + TABLES

Despite their varied origins, handmade chairs and tables from around the world have a wonderfully timeless quality. First and foremost intended to be functional items, they often possess an elegant simplicity that is perfectly suited to the contemporary home.

Handcrafted chairs have an integrity and appeal that modern mass-produced items can never match. One prized item, whether it is old or new, can make a unique centerpiece, and the robust, expressive lines of a primitive African stool or the elegant form of a classic Chinese chair will combine effortlessly with the clean lines of modern designs or pieces from the 1930s and 1940s.

Occasional tables are always useful, and in Middle Eastern and North African countries, small tables for serving coffee are very common. Usually octagonal in shape, and intricately inlaid with bone or mother of pearl or carved with crisp designs, they were an integral feature of the "Turkish rooms" so popular in Europe in the late 19th century, and look just as good in a contemporary interior. Oriental-style side tables made from bamboo and imitation lacquer were produced in great numbers after Japanese lacquerwork was first seen at the Paris Exhibition of 1867 and, if you are lucky, can sometimes still be found in antique markets and secondhand stores.

Many developing countries produce chunky, robust coffee tables for export, often made from reclaimed wood. Today, woods like ebony and mahogany are seriously endangered, so if you are buying newly made furniture, check that the wood is from a sustainable source. For unusual tables, think creatively. An old chest or African stool can double as a coffee table. Huge cable reels discarded by builders make very serviceable tables, and salvaging such items is just the kind of resourceful recycling that you would find in a developing country.

SITTING IN STYLE *All owned by intrepid travelers, these chairs were brought back from distant lands but are perfectly at home in their new settings. The primitive "thrones" are in daily use and admired for their history as well as their simplicity (above left, center, and opposite). The decorative Chinese chair combines Eastern culture with Western influences (above right).*

STOOLS + BENCHES

SIMPLE SEATING *The simpler the style, the more modern the appeal when it comes to the wooden stools of the African continent. The ovoid form of a 1970s fireplace is balanced by the curves of an African stool and echoed in the circles of a contemporary rug (opposite). Larger pieces can be used as side tables (below), while the tiniest of stools look charming in a group (right).*

Stools and benches are the most simple and basic forms of seating, consisting only of a horizontal surface with supports. Found in homes both grand and humble the world over, they are an economical, easily portable, and endlessly versatile form of seating that can also double as a low table.

Old African stools often boast a wealth of historical associations. Perhaps the most famous are those produced by the Ashanti people of Ghana—low seats without arms or backs and adorned with detailed carving. Tribal chiefs sat in state on their own personal stool, which no one else would dare to sit upon. During the 19th century, Europeans venturing into Africa brought with them their own upholstered chairs, along with other essentials such as gramophones, cut-glass chandeliers, and gilt mirrors. Skilled local carvers were commissioned to make copies of European styles, which, in their turn, influenced local designs. Accordingly, some chiefs' stools were studded with upholstery nails and given arms and a straight back.

It is not only Ashanti chiefs who had their own personal stools. Lesser mortals had "white stools" or *nkonnua fufuo*, which were scrubbed with water and sand, and sometimes lime to bleach them clean. Those who led a blameless and good life could hope to have their stool blackened to become a *nkonnua tuntum*. If this honor was bestowed, the stool was treated with raw egg, soot, and the blood of a sheep. These days, in many less-developed parts of Africa, stools still play an important role. Waiting all day for a bus or train is not unusual, so often people carry their own hand-carved stools in preparation for long roadside waits.

In China, stools first appeared during the Ming dynasty (1368–1644). Elegant and refined, the two classic forms are the barrel-shaped *dun* and the elaborately carved square or rectangular *deng*, which often served as a small table.

Chests and cabinets are essential storage solutions in any home. These versatile items can be used for storing quilts, bedlinen, personal belongings, clothes, and much more, but can also be pressed into service as an extra seat, display space, or table when needed. Produced in great numbers in many different countries around the world, chests and cabinets are an important element of the modern home.

In China, the multitude of migrant traders and workers gave rise to the manufacture of a great array of portable chests and cupboards. Clothes were packed away in chests for long journeys, documents were stashed away safely, and furniture was made to be easy to dismantle. Many Chinese cupboards were built with flush edges so they could be neatly stacked next to each other.

Traditionally, the Japanese used little furniture in their homes, but they did produce a large number of storage chests, known as *tansu*. Japanese lacquered cabinets were one of the most popular items brought to Europe from the Far East from the 17th century on, and the *shodana*, a display cabinet with many asymmetrical small drawers, shelves, and compartments, was produced expressly for the export market. The marriage chest—a chest of drawers made especially for a girl about to marry—was prevalent in both the East and the West until the 19th century, giving rise to the "hope chest."

Handsome, sturdy chests also originate from India and Arab countries, where the traditional nomadic way of life meant that secure and weatherproof containers were neccessary for transporting valuables. Many bear the marks of Islamic style, with brass-headed nails and heavy, ornate hinges similar to those found on the bolted doors of Moroccan palaces. These chests are a good choice for storing away bedlinen, blankets, and out-of-season clothes.

STORAGE

CABINETS *India has a great love of wood. Many of its exports combine old and new, as in the case of these large cabinets (below and right). The old doors, with their metal bars and decorative handles, have been attached to new carcasses in lower-quality wood. In a country where even thatched houses are decorated with mirrors, it is perhaps not surprising to find a cabinet encrusted with them (opposite).*

SIMPLE STORAGE *In a corner of a fashion designer's basement, a hutch of South American origin holds a display of pottery (below). This enormous black lacquered armoire (right) may appear Oriental due to its color and finish, but it is in fact a 1940s Belgian piece and is rightfully at home in this Brussels bedroom. When it comes to storage, a chest or trunk is essential for concealing life's less attractive bits and pieces (opposite). Fabulous baskets and boxes can be found the world over and also make stylish hiding places.*

Indian woodcarving skills were particularly in demand during the days of the British Raj, when foreign settlers commissioned native woodworkers to produce European-style pieces of furniture to make them feel at home while abroad. Today, styles that are more obviously Indian—inset with tiny mirrors or differently colored wood or decorated with intricate carvings—are more appreciated. But even an inexpensive chest of drawers or a tacky old armoire can be given a global flavor by adding colorful glass doorknobs or a lick of paint in a bright jewel shade.

Baskets are used for storage the world over—for carrying firewood, transporting goods to market, or moving belongings over large distances. In a modern home, they are no less useful. Baskets can contain or conceal a multitude of objects—bedlinen, magazines, or firewood—while smaller stacking baskets can hold kitchen or bathroom nicknacks, plants, or stationery. Strong and sturdy, flexible or rigid, made from materials such as sisal or wicker, baskets can be found in a selection of natural hues or interwoven with brightly colored dyed fibers.

Light is essential—it is needed to make our surroundings visible—but at the same time, it has a strong effect on our moods and emotions. In much of the world, home lighting, almost exclusively, means electric light. In the West, we are fortunate to have access to constant illumination at the flick of a switch—a convenience few of us would permanently exchange for the evocative glow of candlelight or the novelty of a kerosene lamp. However, lamps and lighting inspired by styles around the world offer an opportunity to add authentic global touches. And for atmospheric, romantic illumination, turn to the most basic form of artificial lighting—candles.

lamps + lighting

SHINE ON *Candles, with their fabulous atmospheric flicker, have enjoyed renewed popularity in recent years. These impressive orbs were brought back from Turkey (opposite). Venetian glass chandeliers are on show in a silver-lined apartment (above left). A vellum light is decorated with henna (above right).*

In many developing countries, lighting is not intended to create special effects or to be deliberately atmospheric—it is an essential element that allows people to stay up after darkness has fallen. In tropical climates, night brings with it a welcome coolness, and people tend to make the most of it by using this time for cooking, carrying out household chores, and sitting up late to share in food and conversation. In many parts of the globe, remote homes without electricity still rely on candlelight or kerosene lamps, while others own a Coleman lamp—a lantern that gives out a fierce white glare.

Historically, early forms of lighting around the world drew on whatever local materials were available. The first lamps in seafaring areas, for example, consisted of a wick laid in the body of an oily fish—the oil would seep into the wick and give out a no doubt rather odiferous but still effective light. In South America, the native Amerindians caught huge glowing humming beetles and used them as a light source, while in Japan, fireflies were trapped in wood and paper cages to provide an evening's worth of light.

The Orient has a long tradition of lanterns crafted from materials such as paper, silk, parchment, and vellum. Today, contemporary versions of the classic Oriental lantern include crumpled paper or parchment shades and oversized paper lanterns in a variety of shapes and sizes. These fixtures screen the light source and create a gentle, diffused glow. Tasseled Chinese lanterns bring the exotic flavor of Chinatown into modern apartments. They are cheap and cheerful, and show a lighter, more frivolous side of global style.

The classic circular lampshade was prevalent in Persia long before it reached the rest of the world, and its descendant is the ubiquitous paper lampshade that has hung aloft in homes around the world since the 1960s. There is now a wide selection of innovative designs and shapes to choose from, from organic curves to modernist cubes that look particularly effective when stacked.

The most basic form of lighting is candlelight. Candles have a special significance in many cultures, and superstitions abound concerning their flickering flames. In the modern

home, candlelight possesses an intimate, homey charm. Natural materials like shells, stone, or wood can be used as simple candleholders. Even today, when seminomadic people of the Egyptian desert make camp in the shelter of an outcrop of boulders, they lodge candles in the fissures of the rock face. Similarly, Pacific islanders use coconut shells or seashells to hold candles. Broad, flat stones or those that have been hollowed out by the sea make attractive candleholders, either for indoors or sheltered areas outside. Decorative shells brought back as mementoes of exotic vacations also make good candleholders.

Moorish-style star-shaped glass lanterns provide a bold focal point in any room and are available in lighting stores. Traditional Moroccan mosque lanterns echo the shapes of Arab arches and minarets, and are usually four-sided or octagonal. Brass or bronze lanterns are often decorated with filigree, or have different-colored panels of glass that only come to life when the lantern is lit. These lanterns often flank the main doors of a mosque, as the *Koran* compares the light of a lamp to the light of God. They also represent the illuminating nature of learning, as from the 13th century mosques were centers of study as well as worship.

LIGHTING STYLES *Successful lighting is both a science and an art. However, on a purely style-concious level, there is a wealth of global designs that can enhance a room. The dramatic Moorish glass star (opposite left) is a oversized modern version of those found in Moroccan souks. A stack of oriental paper and bamboo shades hangs among the multicultural furniture found in a Paris apartment (opposite center), while the graphic lines of this modern lamp empathize with the oriental chest it sits on (opposite right). More inexpensive and fun are decorated and tasseled paper lanterns (this page, above), such as those hung in the windows of a New York advertising agency (above right). They also make atmospheric outdoor lighting on balmy nights (above left).*

METAL + GLASS *Tableware that has stood the test of time is ideal for everyday use. Superbly worked and virtually indestructible, Indian metalware develops an engaging patina of age (opposite and below left). Every piece of recycled glass has the charm of being truly individual (left). These squat teapots (below right) are so beguiling their owner can't get enough of them!*

kitchenware + tableware

Global kitchenware and tableware are a good way to introduce an element of the exotic or the unusual into a contemporary home, for not only do such objects look good, they are also extremely practical. Whether items are purchased at home or abroad, are mass-produced or handcrafted, prices are often very reasonable, especially for more utilitarian pieces, so it is easy and quick to build up a collection of different kitchenware and tableware for everyday use or decorative purposes.

The popularity of all things Eastern means that nowadays department stores are just as good a hunting ground for oriental tableware as any exotic vacation destination. The items arrayed on this table (below and opposite) are a mixture of modern mass-produced ceramics and pieces handmade by a ceramicist who is greatly influenced by ancient oriental ceramics. The rich blue bowl (left) was made in Morocco but purchased in a gift shop closer to home.

In India, kitchenware is usually made from metal, because it is long-lasting and virtually unbreakable. Beaten copper and brass are traditionally used for cookware, but cheaper aluminum and stainless steel also abound; and bell metal, an alloy of copper and tin with an attractive golden sheen, is also popular. The Indian subcontinent's diverse cultures and food traditions mean there is a huge selection of differently sized and shaped cooking pots. New Indian cooking pots have an unexpectedly shiny, streamlined look and are best seen in action, cooking homemade curries and sauces. Older Indian cooking pots, often possessing a pleasing patina of age due to years of intensive use, are now better used as decorative items.

Factories and mass-production methods have now replaced traditional glassblowing methods almost everywhere, but in Mexico small village furnaces, where broken glass and old bottles are melted down and recycled into new pieces, still exist. The chunky, robust handcrafted glasses these furnaces produce are often shot with needlepoints and bubbles, or are purposefully given a crackle effect by dunking them in cold water immediately after blowing. Mexican glasses are often tinted green (from copper) or have a yellow tinge (from iron), and make stylish yet inexpensive buys and excellent presents.

Much modern ceramic work from around the world has its roots in the ancient porcelain of China. From the 12th century on, a huge range of vessels, including bowls, teapots, and vases, were produced for each emperor's court, the decoration and quality becoming increasingly more refined due to technical developments and to impress successive rulers.

WOODEN OBJECTS *In many African cultures, kitchen items and utensils symbolize femininity and fertility, and are made in the shape of a woman. These heavy South African chopping blocks (opposite) are exceptions—they are in the shape of men! Kenyan salad servers made especially for the tourist market are decorated with batik-style prints (above left). Wooden vessels originally used to hold oil or milk enjoy a new lease on life in a global kitchen (above right).*

By the 15th century, courtly potters at imperial kilns were creating richly colored glazes of yellow, ruby red, and a bold blue from cobalt. When traders first brought Chinese blue and white porcelain to Europe, it had an enormous influence on Islamic and European craftsmen, resulting in the blue and green glazes of Islamic tiling, Delft tiles in the Netherlands, and English willow-pattern crockery. However, European manufacturers were frustrated in their efforts to achieve the same translucent quality as the Chinese—by the 18th century, some Chinese porcelain was as thin as eggshell. White porcelain clay needs an experienced hand, as potters say it has a "memory" and pots can carry on twisting in the direction they have been thrown during firing. Despite these technical hurdles, the 18th century witnessed new "china" factories springing up all over Europe, from Meissen in Germany to Wedgwood's pottery in Staffordshire, England.

Today, the East and Southeast Asia still remain a fertile source of ceramics. The region's history can be seen in the delicate, tapering shapes and an enduring fascination with blue and jade-green glazes. Japanese ceramics were another high art form, with potters being apprenticed to master potters to learn their craft. More robust stoneware or *raku* is also typical of Japan, where the asymmetrical and irregular shapes of *raku* are celebrated for their "imperfect" and rustic feel. This is seen as especially appropriate for tea ceremonies, where anything too highly decorated might spoil the

ZEN STYLE *The idea of a calm and serene oriental-style eating experience appeals to many. A table laid in a sparse, symmetrical fashion (below) keeps clutter to a minimum. Tea time is much more aesthetically pleasing when tea is served from a Chinese-style crackle-glaze pot into simple bowls (opposite). Delicate salt-dough pieces from Afghanistan are made to be admired rather than for heavy use (right).*

contemplative mood. In China, black or deep purple are favored colors for teapots and drinking bowls, as the finest tea turns pure white or bluish gray on infusion, and these colors provide a pleasing contrast. Even if mornings are a rushed affair, tea made in a delicate handmade pot will always be a more pleasant experience than a hastily dunked teabag in a thick mug. For cereal or soup, the mass-produced blue and white rice bowls so typical of Chinese restaurants have a refreshing, everyday appeal, so it is worth rooting through the shelves at Chinese supermarkets and cookware stores.

The easiest and fastest way to make pottery is on a wheel, but more basic techniques such as coiling clay into pots or using a flat paddle to slap the clay into shape around a mold or one's hand are still more usual practice in many places. In developing countries all over the globe, simple handmade pots destined for use as cook- or kitchenware are usually left unglazed, but naive decorations or motifs may be scratched or painted on, sometimes using white or red slip (colored clay thinned with water). The pots are then stacked in the open air, interleaved with cakes of dry cow dung and straw, and baked until they are hard.

RECYCLING *Metal lassi cups, some simple, some highly decorated, are lined up to provide easy access to the cooking paraphernalia they charmingly store (overleaf).*

UTENSILS + BOWLS *Some utensils and spoons are as decorative as they are practical. A still life of a primitive wooden ladle with a modern oriental vase beside it (below) can bring immense pleasure. These cheap aluminum spoons have comical cartoonlike proportions (near right). Humble bowls and spoons possess a utilitarian appeal (far right). When struck with a mallet, these Tibetan singing bowls make beautiful sounds that aid meditation (opposite left). A decorative vessel holds flowerheads (opposite right).*

Wood is used to make pots and bowls in India and Southeast Asia, while gourds from the calabash tree are used as natural vessels in Africa. These round or bottle-shaped fruits (related to the squash family) grow to large sizes and, once the seeds have been scraped out and the gourd left to dry, make handy cups, containers, and water dippers. In Mexico, gourds are fashioned into wide bowls or perforated to make strainers. The people of the Namib desert traditionally engraved and decorated ostrich eggs and used them as water containers, sometimes burying them in the sand for emergency supplies when water was scarce. Much modern African pottery echoes these ovoid, organic shapes and has a tactile, unpretentious feel.

Hardwearing, durable equipment for food preparation is a very practical way of bringing global style into the home. Stone or wooden *paraths*—a kneading bowl used to make flat bread—are a common sight in Rajasthani kitchens, while heavy stone pestles and mortars are used for grinding spices and seeds. Basic robust items like these are worthwhile investments, since they are made to last.

Utensils from around the world can be both decorative and practical. Rice is the staple foodstuff for much of the world, and in many places rice spoons have a particular significance. In Madagascar, for example, such spoons are handed down over generations since rice is seen as sacred and the product of the toil of their ancestors.

The desire to collect seems to be a natural human urge—one that affects everybody, whether they spend hours poring over their collection of antique lace or simply pocket a couple of special shells every time they walk along a beach. Collecting offers a way to put a stamp of individuality on your home and will allow you to unify pieces from totally different times and places. And as a collector, shopping forays abroad take on new meaning: the search is on for that special pair of slippers or miniature coffee cup that will always be a potent reminder of a place and its people. When it comes to displaying collections, be bold and imaginative. Give careful thought to placement and composition, and arrange your treasures where they can be admired and appreciated on a day-to-day basis.

collections

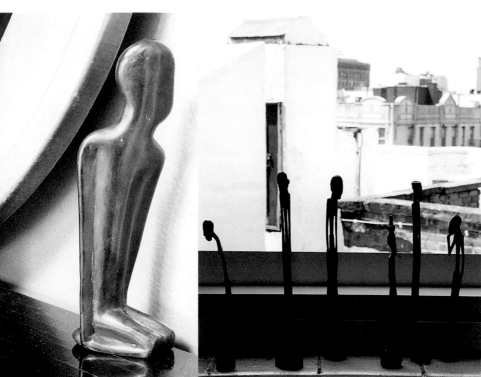

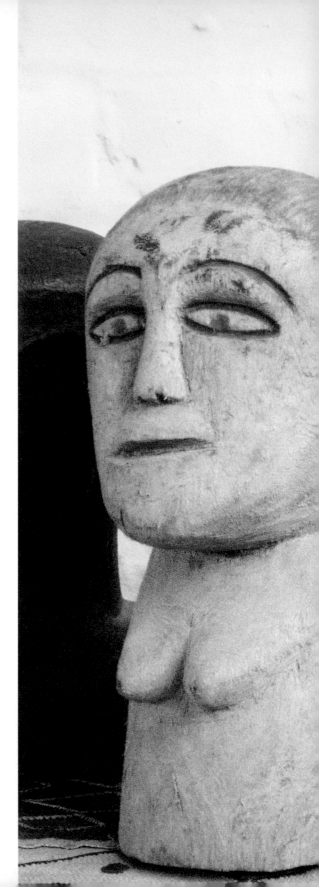

FIGURATIVE *Soapstone figures are something of an export phenomenon, but look carefully and you could find a beautifully simple piece (above left). African carved figures survey the New York skyline (above right). These "ex voto" heads have traveled from a Brazilian chapel to a London home via a New York dealer (opposite).*

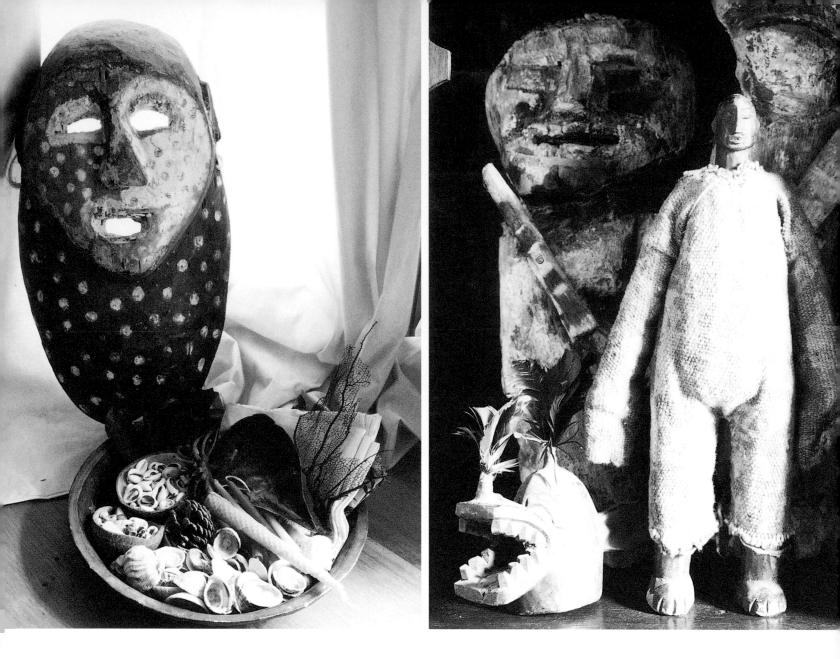

RELIGIOUS OBJECTS

MASKS + FIGURES *One culture's taboo is often another's aesthetic treat! Tribal and ceremonial masks belong to a way of life far removed from the modern world, but can be appreciated for their age and history (above left). This wooden figure (with headdress beside it) was found in a Paris flea market, its origins unknown, and sits on a kitchen shelf with a pair of rough-hewn Mexican companions behind it (above right). Fetish dolls of bone and hair have a surreal charm when casually perched on a window ledge, far removed from Africa and all their sinister implications (opposite left). Paddy, the Jack Russell, is oblivious to the liberal mix of Catholic statuettes and primitive wooden figures displayed just behind him (opposite right).*

The trappings of people's beliefs from around the world provide a rich source of collectables. Objects ranging from plastic statuettes of biblical characters to powerful hand-carved masks make unique and fascinating ornaments.

Dolls and masks from Africa represent powerful beliefs that are just as strong as mainstream religions. Fetish dolls are small sculptures with a space reserved to hold a "medicine" or "magical" substance, usually a hollow in the stomach or a horn on the head. Each doll has a purpose, usually quite benign, such as protection from disease. Once the medicine is removed, the dolls are no longer needed and are often sold to collectors.

The *akua ba* dolls of the Ashanti people of Ghana have a positive influence: they are carried by expectant mothers in the belief that if they look only upon objects of beauty, their child will be beautiful, too. The dolls have long necks and round, flat faces, expressing the Ashanti ideal of beauty. Many African sculptures or dolls are shaped like infants, with large heads and short legs, because newborns are believed to be spiritually close to ancestors.

Certain artefacts are associated with the darker side of life: some masks are worn in ceremonies to call up the spirits of ancestors or to root out sorcerers. In small villages, a mask also means a dancer can leave his public face behind and take on a different role. Other carvings are linked with the afterlife. Wooden funerary posts from Kenya are placed near a newly filled-in grave to provide a temporary home for a restless spirit until it is ready to go

RELIGIOUS *Many collectors share a fascination with all things spiritual or ecclesiastical. Imagery of angels is popular, probably due to their serene quality. Global collections are often an eclectic affair, so it is not unusual to see a crucifix with a Buddha nearby (opposite left) or an angel beside a primitive Indian goddess (opposite right). Tableaux (below) are also popular collectors' items—this tin example (far left) lights up while angels rotate at high speed. Superstition can dictate the maintaining of such shrines as this one in a New York office (left), but one can't help feeling that its kitsch quality is the true source of its appeal!*

MANY COLLECTORS SHARE A FASCINATION WITH ALL THINGS SPIRITUAL OR ECCLESIASTICAL

on its way. The Aborigines produce similar grave markers called *tutini*, which represent the deceased and show an unbreakable bond with their forefathers.

Household shrines are common in homes across Asia, where the day begins with offerings for the gods. Sculptures of Buddha are placed at a raised level to indicate that he is removed from ordinary people and to draw the eyes to Buddha's hands, which are carefully placed to signify composure. Hands are also a focus of Hindu statues: placed together, they signify prayer, and when held upward, they represent peace. Today, carvers at pilgrimage sites offer replicas of temple statues, and it is often possible to discover something that truly recalls the spirit of the originals.

When the Spaniards colonized Latin America, they brought with them the evocative and colorful images of Catholicism that can be seen in churches and homes today. Some shrines echo the small portable altar boxes or *retablos* containing miniaturized biblical scenes that the Spanish brought with them to South America for converting the "heathen." Despite the spread of Catholicism, Mexicans also clung fast to their own beliefs, and they still celebrate the Day of the Dead by picnicking on their ancestors' graves and decorating their homes with tin or papier-mâché skeletons. However, the mood tends to be festive and hedonistic rather than ghoulish, and mementoes of *Dia de los Muertos* fittingly capture Mexico's exuberant, wild side.

BUTTONS AND BEADS *Cowrie shells, beads, and buttons adorn hats worn by the Kuba and Warega people of Zaire (overleaf, left). The beaded items are made by the Masai, who have almost forty different words to describe types of beadwork (right).*

SHOES

COLLECTING *The modern global collector need not be too concerned about whether something is "genuine" or "antique," as long as it pleases the eye. It may be a reminder of exotic bazaars visited on a fabulous far-flung vacation or, as is the case with much of this collection of decorative shoes, bought in yard sales and local flea markets without even leaving home turf. Footwear from around the world makes an attractively different collection. Some shoes are miniature works of art, like these tiny Chinese slippers with intricate embroidery detail (second from right, bottom row). Exotic styles are not confined to women and children. In northwestern India, fancy pointed slippers, or jootis, are worn by men, while Moroccan men slip on similar babouches. The miniature Turkish slippers (second from left, top row) came from an airport souvenir shop.*

JEWELRY

All around the world, jewelry has evolved into a way to display one's wealth and status—and simultaneously keep it safe. For the nomadic people of North Africa and India, their heavy silver bracelets and necklaces were the portable equivalent of a bank account. In India, chokers or *hansi* that bear the image of a god are also worn as lucky charms to protect the body against illness, and are sported by men as well as women. In Moorish countries, lucky amulets or charms are similarly worn to ward off the evil eye, which is regarded as an ever-present force to be guarded against.

Ivory, bone, or white plastic bangles encircle the arms of women from Rajasthan. This tells the world that a woman is married and has moved to her husband's family home, and the bangles will remain on her arms until her husband dies. In Indian emporiums there is a bewildering assortment of rings, bracelets, chokers, earrings, and toe rings (intended to be worn by married women only) to choose from. Many such pieces, in gold or silver, are given

to a bride before her marriage, a tradition that dates back to the time when a Hindu woman's only property in the eyes of the law was her dowry jewelry.

Beads were treasured by the Africans as a source of currency and as a sign of status and wealth. Shaka, the 19th-century king of the Zulus, was such a great bead lover that he decreed that any new beads brought into the region be shown to him so he could decide whether or not to keep them for himself. Nowadays, antique African beaded jewelry is highly collectible, but modern pieces can be found in many craft markets.

Handcarved antique ivory, bone, or wood bangles possess undeniable textural appeal, as does the dull sheen of old silver. But handfuls of inexpensive glittering glass bangles are just as nice a way to bring home memories of another country. As a collection builds up, it will reveal remarkable similarities of shape and material in jewelry from very different nations. For added pleasure, keep an eye out for pieces that can be worn on special occasions.

ADORNMENTS *Necklaces
and beads come in a multitude of
materials—glass, shell, bone,
metal, woven fibers, hair, stone,
and wood—the list is extensive.
When we look in delight and
amazement at antique jewelry
from all around the world, we have
to appreciate their preconservation
use of the likes of ivory and shell,
despite understanding that the
modern use of such materials
would be unacceptable.*

FLOWER COLLECTION

PICKING FLOWERS *A vase of hothouse flowers might look exotic, but for year-round blooms that really capture the spirit of a country, fake it. Wire, shell, silk, paper, and plastic are among the materials used to fashion fake flowers for little or no cost. In a country where nothing goes to waste, South Africans recycle soft-drink cans into tin flowers, complete with the logos resplendent on the petals. This ingenuity stems from necessity, but also shows a creative spirit undampened by hardship.*

Mexican cantinas and kitchens hum with color, and a bunch of shocking pink flowers adds extra zing. If they last a year instead of a week, that makes them even better value. In northern Thailand, a small women's cooperative has won a local award for turning out mulberry paper flowers with each petal carefully cut and tinted to look like the genuine article. But for the modern global home, it is not so important whether fake flowers are realistic or not. In fact, an ersatz quality can be a definite bonus, giving a kitsch appeal. Collecting fake flowers makes good sense: they are light to carry home from abroad, reflect the popular culture of a country, and what's more, they'll never wilt.

LIVING SPACES/ KITCHENS + EATING AREAS/ BEDROOMS/
BATHROOMS/WORKSPACES/GARDENS + GARDEN ROOMS

rooms

ALLOW EAST AND WEST, NORTH AND SOUTH TO MEET AND YOU WILL CREATE A

A country's colors, surfaces, textiles, furniture, and everyday ephemera are part of its integral character, but it is only when these elements are combined that global style comes to life, creating inspiring and imaginative rooms that are a pleasure to live, relax, and work in.

When creating a global home, the aim is not to slavishly replicate a Japanese dining room, for example, or a Moroccan bedroom—such a regimented "painting by numbers" approach, where everything matches, leaves little room for experimentation and inventiveness. Instead, global style allows you to incorporate hand-crafted Indian furniture, African pottery, or exotic Chinese silks with 18th-century French antiques or Scandinavian modern classics.

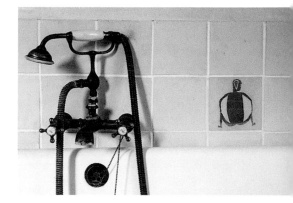

GLOBALLY INSPIRED HOME THAT IS ENTIRELY UNIQUE

Allow east and west, north and south to meet and you will create a globally inspired home that is entirely unique. Exotic elements can come together to create comfortable and versatile living rooms and kitchens, tranquil bedrooms enlivened with individual touches, bathrooms influenced by bathing rituals from around the world, and home workspaces that are truly inspiring. And, as much of life in hot or tropical climates takes place outside, cleverly designed gardens and garden rooms can bring the tropics a little closer to home. With global style, there is no right or wrong way to decorate—this imaginative and liberating approach means anyone can create a home that will suit their lifestyle while reflecting a passion for the exotic and eclectic.

In modern homes, most day-to-day activities—eating, relaxing, and entertaining—take place in one main room, and therefore it is important that the surroundings are both comfortable and stylish. Inspired use of color, texture, and furnishings will help to set the scene and create the desired effect, whether it be minimalist and understated or rich and dramatic. And if you only want to introduce a hint of the exotic, incorporate carefully chosen global elements with existing furniture and furnishings to create living spaces that are a pleasure to spend time in.

living spaces

A HOME OF ONE'S OWN *A room can be enriched by adding a couple of global touches—a scattering of cushions (above right) or an exotic pot for plants or flowers (above left), while others may embrace the concept and enjoy developing a more all-encompassing global theme (opposite).*

CALMING NEUTRALS AND SHADES OF WHITE WILL CREATE AN UNDERSTATED BACKDROP FOR TREASURES FROM DISTANT LANDS

Bringing global style to your living space calls for a light touch, as living rooms were the scenes of some of the worst excesses of hippy chic in the 1960s and 1970s. Even though colors, furnishings, and textiles from around the globe are undeniably beautiful, resist the temptation to amass piles of rugs, wall hangings, and trinkets. Instead, keep things clean and light, in tune with a contemporary interior, and do not let your exotic treasures take over.

Color is an extremely evocative element of any interior. It influences mood, creates atmosphere, and is reminiscent of exotic destinations and different cultures. In living areas, calming neutrals and shades of white on walls and floors and at windows will create an understated backdrop for treasures from distant lands, such as richly colored rugs and carpets, boldly patterned textiles, unusual masks or carvings, and quirky pieces of furniture. However, if you

LOW-LEVEL LIVING *is a traditional part of several cultures. Today, its simplicity and sophistication gives it a wider appeal. These three examples are very different in feel, but all center on the low table to eat from and lounge around. A rattan bed frame from the Philippines is used as a coffee table in a New York apartment (above left). Giant floor cushions are made from vintage kimonos (above center). A low table is surrounded by traditional mats for reclining upon (opposite).*

ORIENTAL EXPRESSION *This
Tribeca loft (this page and opposite)
pays tranquil homage to Oriental
simplicity with a few contemporary
twists. The ceiling undulates in a
soothing wave, while the shiny exposed
pipework adds a hint of industrial chic.
Everything else in the room could be
packed up in a matter of seconds. The
opaque screening that forms an alcove
around the Chinese scholar's desk is
movable and flexible, while the heavier
bookcase screens can be reconfigured
into different arrangements. The two
specially commissioned heavy-weave
natural fibre rugs denote the designated
eating and living areas.*

yearn for a more vibrant scheme, let color be the central focus of the room and adopt a more restrained approach to furnishings and ornaments. Bold colors such as tropical aquamarine or fiery crimson add drama, while rich, intense shades such as turmeric yellow, burnt orange, or deep turquoise are strong yet muted and exude tranquility.

Textiles are another good way to inject color into a living room. Allow warming, woven textiles in rich red, brown, and other earthy shades to be the central focus in a room—a special kilim or carpet hung on the wall will get the attention it deserves in a neutral environment, but surrounded by equally rich shades, it is in danger of being drowned out.

Fabrics from around the world bring interest and a hint of the exotic to the living room. Exuberantly printed African or Indian textiles or shimmering oriental silk can be used as upholstery fabrics and to cover pillows, so their texture can be enjoyed as well as their colors. To emphasize different textures, play around with contrast and place opposites together—rough brickwork beside smooth glass, or brittle slate next to the sheen of satin—so a living room becomes a tactile as well as a visual experience.

Light also affects mood and atmosphere, and has great creative potential. Natural light provides variety and diversity, and adds vitality to an interior, so let as much flow in as possible, and do not block it with thick curtains or dark blinds. Artificial lighting should create interest, enhance decoration and heighten atmosphere. A basic installation of central or ceiling fixtures can be supplemented by additional fixtures. Spotlights can focus attention on favorite pieces, while wall and floor lights will provide scope for many different combinations. Furnishing a living room is an ideal opportunity to seek out unusual lampshades and lanterns from around the world.

A QUIET CORNER *This late 19th-century chair by Joseph Fenby (opposite) was originally designed for high-ranking officers to take on military campaigns. Its aged leather gives it a colonial air, which is reinforced by the African fabric pillow, the classic louvered doors, and the lush tropical garden beyond. It is the odd pieces dotted around a room that say global (left). A fashion stylist brought back this fine cowrie shell container, a string of seed pod beads, and even a framed scorpion from her trips to Kenya. The generously sized floor pillows are modern, but primitive in spirit.*

IN THE RED *Red can bring an exotic element to a living room. In this London interior, a deep red concrete floor and rough-hewn walls bring a sense of primitive simplicity (opposite). A Thai bench, Indian cushions, and a statuesque cactus continue the global theme. In an ancient Paris apartment, the original beams have been painted a bold red, creating a Chinese atmosphere (below right). Other strong colors can be just as dynamic— here sunshine spills on to bold blue walls in a London bathroom (right).*

When choosing furniture, adopt a bold approach and mix and match items from around the globe. To make sure styles complement each other, keep color schemes simple and avoid an excess of ornate shapes and fussy patterns. A dark wooden African chair, for example, will sit happily beside other seats if they are made from similar woods or share an economy of line or simplicity of form.

Every living room needs an inviting sofa to flop on, the bigger the better. Alternatively, in many countries, relaxing, entertaining, and eating are low-level activities that take place on cushions or mats on the ground or low platforms. In Central Asia, for example, teahouses are furnished with low platforms strewn with cushions, providing inviting surroundings for customers to recline on. If floor-level lounging appeals, invest in a low table to set the scene. Furniture specialists import such tables from countries like India, Indonesia, and Africa, and buying here is easier than arranging for an item to be shipped home. A chunky, solid table will serve you well for decades, gaining character over the years.

For a more pared-down, minimalist feel, take inspiration from the traditional Japanese interior. Briefly hijacked by hardheaded corporate design in the 1980s, Japanese style can in fact create a serene, tranquil, and very contemporary environment. Simple furniture shapes add to the streamlined, understated effect, and there are no superfluous clutter or ornaments to distract the eye. Japanese interiors use screens to subdivide space and mark off areas for different activities. Adopt this versatile idea and choose a screen that is in keeping with the rest of the room—Japanese-style wood and rice paper, bamboo, slatted wood, or even sandblasted glass.

Details bring a room to life, and delight and intrigue the eye, which is where ornaments like carvings, masks, or pottery come in. Do not feel constrained into displaying objects by country or by theme, such as a side table of African animal carvings or a mantelpiece lined with color-coordinated oriental ceramics. Instead, adapt a more lateral and imaginative approach. Gather together favorite pieces that share a similiar form, subject matter, or color. Experiment with different arrangements and groupings, then stand back and admire your handiwork. Colorful batik or silk cushions, handcrafted basketware from Africa and the Far East, pieces of antique ethnic jewelry from India and North Africa, odd driftwood and beautiful shells collected on foreign beaches, African soapstone sculptures, and chunky primitive pottery and carvings are all fascinating artefacts well worthy of display space, and they will also bring back memories of trips abroad or evoke different cultures.

If you yearn for a jungly tropical effect, lots of foliage and plants are the answer. If your garden is visible from the living room, so much the better, but in a high-rise city apartment, bring the outside in with a collection of bold and exotic plants such as black-stemmed bamboo.

COMFORTABLY ECLECTIC

In this London living space, carefully combined global pieces picked up on travels or from local flea markets create elegant still lifes (opposite page). Meanwhile, over the Atlantic, the owner of this Manhattan pied-à-terre has adopted a similarly eclectic approach (left and below). The walls are silver and the floor a slick black. Pieces from different periods and countries make up the furnishings. The message is have the confidence to do your own thing and ignore the dictates of ever-changing fashions.

KITCHENS + EATING AREAS *Fun and funky, a global kitchen can carry cheap and cheerful artefacts with great style and panache. Quirky and unexpected elements like a recycled Chinese honeypot used as a vase, a coolie-hat lampshade, and an Oriental screen add a touch of the exotic.*

kitchens + eating areas

In many countries, the kitchen is an area that is no longer solely dedicated to the preparation of food but is now at the very heart of family life. The demise of the formal dining room has led to the kitchen's becoming a living and eating area, so its design and decoration has become more important. Bringing global elements to kitchen and dining areas offers an opportunity to break away from more traditional or expected styles and create welcoming rooms that have plenty of individuality and character without sacrificing any convenience or home comforts.

For global kitchen and eating areas, combine a variety of influences to create rooms that are modern and convenient, but with an imaginative and exotic flavor. For the perfect result, mix and match furniture and fixtures from around the world—smooth, cool Moroccan tiles with Japanese paper blinds, rush matting next to cheap Chinese lanterns—for a funky, eclectic feel. Collect colorful cookware, handmade dishes, and exotically packaged foodstuffs to adorn shelves and worksurfaces. The overall effect should be warm, welcoming, and relaxing—a laidback kitchen that is a pleasure to linger in.

Unexpected textures and strong colors will bring a global flavor to a modern kitchen. In Mexico, kitchens are often painted a cobalt blue shade called *azul anul* that is believed to ward off evil spirits. Variations on the blue theme, from deep turquoise through to aqua and jade, are refreshing shades for kitchens, while the candy colors of the Caribbean— fondant pink, heady lilac, and pistachio green—will create a more retro 1950s feel. Alternatively, the rich terracottas, ochers, and sandy hues associated with

KITCHEN CULTURE *The tiles and lighting give this elegant kitchen (left, above and opposite) a distinctly Moroccan feel. The coolly sophisticated effect is tempered by the Chinese silk tea cozies and quirky mismatched doorknobs. Indian ceramic drawer pulls sit happily alongside African-inspired iron handles designed by the kitchen's owner (opposite).*

SET IN STONE *This apartment, in an ancient building on Paris's Left Bank, is resolutely uncompromised by its age and history (this page and opposite). Even the ceiling beams have been painted an irreverent tomato red. The kitchen consists of a concrete carcass, finished on the work surfaces with the designer's signature inset stonework, and Indian metal cutout screen doors. Gridlike shelving holds Moroccan pottery and other kitchen accouterments.*

the African landscape will evoke a more welcoming and cozy atmosphere, ideal for a kitchen with a large dining room or where a great deal of entertaining takes place.

The materials chosen for the main surfaces in a kitchen will dictate the overall character of the room. Ceramic tiles possess a cool, sleek finish, and in a hot climate provide a cool and hygienic work surface. They work particularly well as splashbacks or even as a large-scale wallcovering. The gleam of stainless steel gives a streamlined, utilitarian feel, while the open grain and mellow tones of wood are homey and relaxed. Polished stone or marble are luxurious materials and tend to be

costly, but are excellent choices for hardwearing floors and work surfaces. If stone is out of your price range, consider concrete. A truly global modern material, concrete has an unconventional and unpretentious charm and is also very practical due to its durability and resilience. However, it must be sealed to make it resistant to water and food stains.

In a developing country, built-in kitchens are out of the reach of most people, and cabinets and chests are used to store food, dishes, and kitchenware. Freestanding kitchens are a good model for the global home—they are relaxed and inviting, as well as being inexpensive and versatile. One-of-a-kind cabinets, hutches, and old food

KITSCH KITCHENS *Adding humor to the kitchen makes household chores pass with a smile. Perched beside a gas burner, a bottle-top figure holds matches (below). An impressive row of faux-Oriental tea caddies (right). A funky plexiglass clock sits beside the salvaged glass edging of a stainless-steel sink (opposite). Venetian glass and 1950s ceramics add to the eclectic mix. A money box in the form of a rosy Oriental girl and her papier-mâché Mexican friends stand on guard beside a cookie tin (inset opposite).*

lockers provide excellent storage conditions for food and kitchen equipment, while a large kitchen table or a butcher's block offer surfaces for food preparation. If space or budget is limited, transform existing built-in units by adding new doors, mismatching knobs, or a quick lick of paint in a vibrant hue.

Cookware and tableware are usually kept on display in global kitchens, rather than hidden away behind closed doors. Kitchenware, utensils, and attractively packaged foodstuffs can be stacked on shelves or piled high in hutches and cupboards. Displaying a row of shiny Indian cooking pots or a collection of Moroccan terracotta tagines is attractive as well as practical. And purely decorative ceramics and glassware can take their place alongside more practical items. On exotic vacations, keep your eyes open for unusual and attractive pieces that will bring flashes of brilliant color or interest to a kitchen.

Modern kitchens are increasingly becoming a place for informal socializing and dining. If there is enough room, eating in the kitchen is practical and easy, and creates a relaxed, casual atmosphere that is conducive to convivial occasions. If you prefer a more self-contained eating area, which also lends itself to formal dining, set aside a corner of your kitchen and create a sense of separation from the main space. Giving a dining area a different floorcovering, for example, will create a visual rather than a physical divider. Screens can provide a stronger sense of delineation and are practical and flexible, allowing for more intimacy or openness as required. Lighting can also demarcate space. In dining areas, it should be dimmable to create a more intimate atmosphere, whereas kitchen areas require good task lighting to illuminate cooking and food preparation activities.

KITCHENS + DINING AREAS *In the basement kitchen of an exceptional fashion designer (opposite and this page), the feel is truly global. Here, all manner of global artefacts are brought back from inspirational travels to live in a happy melting pot.*

Bedrooms afford the chance to close the door gently on the outside world and let global influences work their magic. Colors can soothe or revitalize, and textiles add luxury, while the bed itself can inspire dreams of distant lands. Whether a mat on the floor or an elaborate four-poster, the bed is a sanctuary the world over, a place to feel safe and to rest after a hard day's work. The bedroom should be decorated with pieces that are beautiful to see upon retiring and rising, and objects should take their cues from the centerpiece—the bed.

bedrooms

DETAILS *Subtle additions to a bedside can add a global flavor—a pair of love dolls (above), a piece of African batik paired with a Colombian mug (right), or an antique 18th-century Chinese side table (opposite).*

A VAST BED, LOOSELY DRAPED WITH FABULOUS
     BEDCLOTHES AND LARGE PILLOWS, IS SURROUNDED
BY A WEALTH OF BEAUTIFUL POSSESSIONS

Bed types and styles vary the world over. In Papua New Guinea, wooden headrests were once carved with a pair of eyes to guard the sleeper from evil spirits as he slept. In Africa, small, carved headrests were seen as signs of status. Not only did they support the head so that elaborate hairstyles remained undisturbed at night, they also provided a means for sleeping and therefore dreaming, which was believed to bring closer contact with the ancestors.

More lavish beds, like canopied beds or four-posters draped with netting, often represented an ostentatious display of wealth rather than a means to keep warm or keep out insects and vermin. Antique Chinese beds, for instance, made from a solid platform with posts at each end and canopied with curtains, were the exclusive preserve of noblemen. India's colonial past produced large four-poster beds draped with Indian cotton or mosquito netting. India is also home to wonderfully decadent swinging beds and chairs that are suspended from chains or thick rope, and day beds that beg to be lazed on during hot, sultry afternoons.

A colonial-style bed is something of an escapist fantasy, whether antique or recreated with gauzy drapes concealing a more modern construction. Many ornately carved colonial styles are copies of European pieces that were reinterpreted by local carvers, a practice that led to a gradual merging of Eastern and Western styles. The early Spanish colonists in countries such as Mexico and Peru at first imported fine

SLEEPING SPACES *A sense of Zenlike calm permeates the bedroom of this pristine Tribeca loft (above). All is neat and precise, with the color scheme limited to a few subdued shades. Well-chosen pieces of furniture and ornaments reinforce the Oriental theme, and the Erin Parrish painting on the wall contributes to the tranquil effect (above left and right). More feminine and exotic is this multicultural bedroom (opposite) with its sumptuous mix of pieces found on world travels. A vast bed, loosely draped with fabulous bedclothes and large pillows, is surrounded by a wealth of beautiful possessions. The effect is relaxed and sensuous.*

furniture from Spain, but a local craft tradition quickly developed, and by the mid-17th century, distinctive colonial styles had evolved. Furniture tended to be European in structure and form, but decoration was influenced by local traditions. Powerful traders like the British East India Company were also responsible for commissioning furniture from indigenous craftsmen. Nowadays, sturdy and durable wooden bedsteads and headboards from India or Indonesia are reassuring in their solidity and are guaranteed to become family heirlooms of the future.

Today, bedrooms in rural or developing areas around the globe are characterized by their simplicity. An Indian bedroom might have beds made from a basic wooden base with a webbing of coir rope to support a mattress. In many countries, woven mats make a practical and portable sleeping surface that is neatly rolled up every morning.

In Morocco, grand brass bedsteads were much coveted by noblemen, providing a lavish centerpiece for a bedchamber lined with rugs and cushioned sofas. Turkish bedrooms were also traditionally havens of comfort and opulence. The Ottoman Empire gave its name to a type of sofa, while the word divan comes from the Turkish council meetings that took place on cushions on a low platform. The opulent look is evocative and escapist, but it benefits from some restraint; otherwise, it can be overwhelming. It is best to choose one or two areas with which to make a statement rather than attempt to make an impact on all fronts: boldly colored walls or exotic bedcovers are both good options.

The pale neutrals of the Orient are particularly suitable for creating a restful bedroom environment. Pure white walls and crisp bedlinen teamed with blond wood and rush matting will give a tranquil and serene effect. This look is not compatible with clutter, so make sure you include plenty of storage space. In a large bedroom or loft, a screen positioned at the head of the bed can separate the sleeping area and create a feeling of safety and protection. Similar alcoves are a feature of Japanese architecture, and in Japanese teahouses a recess called a *tokonoma* acts as a refuge or a place in which to forget the public face and recover the private self—not so very different to the recuperative nature of the modern bedroom.

BEDROOMS *In the guest bedrooms of both these London houses, a neutral color scheme is enlivened by the use of strong pattern. A batik cloth acts as a bedspread (left) and harmonizes with the bold stripes of a kilim on the floor. The sloping eaves hold shelves packed with paper dress patterns, giving a clue to the owner's occupation of fashion designer. In her own bedroom, the owner displays her diaphanous designs on a tribal spear (below). This paneled room (opposite left and right) combines English furniture with a collection of African fabrics bought on trips to Kenya.*

A bedroom is the most intimate and personal room in the house, and the objects that decorate it should reflect this—display old family photographs, cherished possessions, and favorite books. Bedrooms also offer an opportunity to indulge a passion for exotic textiles. Spangly embroidered or mirrored Indian cloth, richly colored or boldly patterned African fabrics, or intricate Indonesian batik can all be used as bedcovers, while swathed and draped lengths of voile bring a hint of colonial charm. On the floor, choose a natural fiber such as jute or sisal, or scatter handmade rugs or kilims that are soft and warm beneath bare feet.

Bedroom lighting needs to be practical—bedside reading lamps, for example, are essential—but it also offers an opportunity to add atmosphere. Light softened by a parchment shade or refracted through a Moroccan-style lantern will create a mellow, sympathetic effect.

No matter how theatrical the decor, bedrooms are first and foremost about indulgence and comfort. One global sleeping style best confined to the garden is the Mexican hammock. Still made by the ancient skill of netting in the Yucatan peninsula, hammocks are ideal for lazy days outside, but sleeping all night in one is definitely an acquired art.

SLEEPING IN STYLE *Private places to indulge the senses— the bedroom can be a discreet haven or a theatrical fantasy. This stunning Portuguese bed (opposite) with its lace-trimmed bedding and mirrored and embroidered antique bedcover dominates a bedroom. This artist's bedroom may look rather like a stage set (above left), but there is something appealing about the eccentricity of it all. An Oriental lacquered day bed (above right) has an extraordinary patchwork cloth on display.*

DREAM ON *Fantastic and indulgent, this magnificent carved and painted four-poster bed swathed in fine white voile (opposite) has a fairy-tale quality that's very appealing. In a compact room in New York (above), a mid-19th century brass bed made up with smooth linen bedding fills one whole wall. It is the addition of the Carlo Bugatti shelf on the silver-painted wall that takes it into the realms of the exotic, along with other global finds such as a Chinese lacquered box perched atop a plastic wine rack. A guest room (left) holds a bed designed by its owner. The calligraphic twisted metal bedhead has an Eastern sensibility, and the theme is continued with intricate Moroccan bedlinen and traditional star lanterns adapted to provide unusual bedside lighting.*

armitage shanks

LIGHT AND AIRY *Global style is extremely compatible with a clean, minimalist look. An ecclesiastical calm pervades this fashion designer's guest bathroom (below left). The chimney breast has been inverted to form an architectural feature with an altarlike effect. The eye is immediately drawn to the two carvings that reside there. The tiles (below right) feature a primitive, African-style motif. In contrast, this Arabian-Nights style bathroom (opposite) offers an exotic vista of colorful tiles, luscious planting, and decorative fretwork.*

bathrooms

The bathroom is necessarily a functional space, but it should also be a relaxing one. Globally inspired bathrooms appeal to all the senses, with tactile surfaces, soothing colors, and scents that evoke indulgent bathing rituals from around the world. Use global elements—natural materials, unusual artefacts, and exotic colors—to add interest and color to a bathroom, and change a potentlally utilitarian space into a uniquely personal retreat. Many bathrooms can be sterile and unwelcoming environments—adding exotic pieces from your travels will make this very important but often neglected room into a relaxing haven that provides a respite from the stresses and strains of everyday life.

Bathing is a personal ritual wherever it takes place, whether it is in the rolltop tub of a colonial-style bathroom or on a shady tropical riverbank. In many hot countries, showering is more common than bathing, as it proves a refreshing antidote to the heat and humidity. In Indonesia, the *mandi* is a deep stone sink kept full to the brim with cool fresh water. The bathers use a dipper fashioned from a dried gourd to shower themselves with scoops of water. In Bali, even the simplest guesthouses have outdoor shower rooms filled with luxuriant vegetation and open to the sun or stars, providing good ventilation and allowing for a sensuous natural bathing experience.

The modern bathing ritual should be a therapeutic affair—a long soak in a warm tub offers an opportunity to soothe away all the day's stresses. Introduce global elements to your bathroom to make bathing an even more escapist experience, choosing textures, objects, and scents that please the senses. Choose a color scheme based around subtle, natural shades, like rich cream, sand, pewter gray, slate blue, and moss green. For surfaces, natural materials such as marble, stone, or slate will evoke the serenity of outdoor bathing and the natural world. Ceramic wall and floor tiles are a more conventional (and very

BATHING IN STYLE *A bathroom with raw concrete walls and wiring protected by plastic switch covers (above and opposite page) combines antique alabaster urns, a 1920s Venetian mirror, and the most unique of "doors"—a vintage Paco Rabanne dress transformed into a curtain of light-catching disks. While the slate surrounds and dark walls of this bathroom (right) could prove oppressive, the extravagant candelabra and sensuous Indian figurines bring the room a lighthearted feel.*

BATHROOMS *A spectacular 300-year-old French copper tub is ensconced in a New York apartment (opposite page). The bathroom is open to the bedroom, and a red Chinese cabinet conceals the usual bathroom paraphernalia. The result is a tranquil idyll that could be a million miles away from the buzz of the Big Apple. In a London bathroom (right), another antique tub goes global with Indian wicker chairs and a head of Buddha. A trio of African combs sit happily beside traditional English hairbrushes (below).*

practical) surface material for bathrooms, but they do not have to be run-of-the-mill in terms of design. Today, tile specialists offer handmade tiles that display plenty of global inspiration in their colors and motifs, and are guaranteed to inject vitality into a modern bathroom.

If space allows, a freestanding bath in the center of the room is a good way to leave the uninspiring layout of the ordinary bathroom behind. Reconditioned rolltop enameled baths or weathered metal hip baths conjure up an indulgent colonial past and can be tracked down in architectural salvage yards, as can old-fashioned chunky sinks and faucets. If what you are looking for proves difficult to track down, many modern manufacturers also produce reproduction "traditional" sanitary ware. If you are on a tight budget or your bathroom is small, a large rolltop bathtub may not be practical. If this is the case, it is easy to dress up a plain white bathtub with reconditioned faucets or other quirky bath fixtures—a few small details can individualize any space, no matter how uninspiring it may seem at first sight. Showering is a practical and economical way to wash, but plastic shower cubicles are sadly lacking in global charm. The global alternative is to construct an enclosed shower area around a central drainage hole and tile it with colorful ceramics.

Decorative items can bring a global flavor to a bathroom. Shells, pebbles, ceramics, or carvings brought back from trips abroad will withstand splashes and steam, as well as acting as reminders of exotic locations—ideal daydream material for long and luxurious soaks.

Working from home is now a reality for many, facilitated by items such as modems, the Internet, and fax machines. Whether your work is creative and requires large work surfaces, drawing boards, and lots of space, or you need nothing more than a computer screen tucked away in a corner, creating the right atmosphere is essential. A home office need not be an imitation of a traditional office. Instead, it offers an opportunity to create a very individual working environment, one that meets your needs in an efficient fashion, while also reflecting your interests and lifestyle.

workspaces

WORKROOMS *A journalist's desk is piled so high with assorted exotica that little room is left for any work to be done (above right and opposite). Organized chaos reigns in this sculptor's studio (above left), where bright tins that once held unusual produce now hold his tools of the trade.*

FAVORITE SOUVENIRS OR HANDCRAFTED ITEMS FROM TRIPS ABROAD CAN
INTRODUCE A MORE DECORATIVE ELEMENT TO A TRADITIONAL-STYLE OFFICE SPACE

Global influences can bring an extra dimension to any home workspace. Favorite souvenirs from trips abroad, along with exotic handcrafted items, can introduce a more decorative element to a traditional-style office space and offer a welcome respite from the hard lines of electronic equipment, while a home office that is entirely kitted out with global furniture, colors, and decorative effects represents a more innovative departure from the conventional office environment.

Any home workspace should be efficient, enjoyable to work in, and conducive to calm concentration. If you do not have enough space to devote a separate room to work, set aside a quiet area with a good source of natural light in which you can accommodate a small work zone. A sense of separation can be created by a change of floorcovering or using storage systems as a screen or dividing line. To decorate your workspace, choose colors that will enliven and energize—red, rich yellow, and warm earth tones—or those that are conducive to calm contemplation—cool gray-green or soothing putty or cream. Take pleasure in avoiding gray, that universally uninspiring shade typical of office environments the world over. There is no reason why a home workspace should not be decorative, imaginative, and a joy to spend time in. Use the walls to display favorite photographs and paintings, and give shelf space to global artefacts or other assorted exotica.

WORKSPACES *Cottage industries with a difference! These work spaces juggle the practical with the decorative in the most imaginative ways. An orderly but colorful workshop (opposite) has a wall of shelves devoted to inspirational finds, while in a book-lined study, Mexican "Day of the Dead" tableaux add a whimsical touch (above left). An Indian dress hangs beside a sewing table in a fashion designer's workshop—the nearby "throne" is piled with fabrics for future creations (above right).*

Plenty of well-planned storage space is essential for any efficient home workspace. Reconditioned office filing cabinets and retail fixtures have a streamlined, industrial appeal, and their weathered appearance gives them more character than bland modern office equipment. For a more relaxed effect, old cupboards or chests from China or India can be used for storage, while a Japanese cabinet could provide a home for stationery or correspondence. Stackable storage boxes or files from business supply stores create an air of efficiency, and can be made more personal and less utilitarian by covering them in African printed fabric or colorful batik. Baskets are an excellent global storage solution. Cheap, durable, and light to carry, they come in all shapes and sizes, and are ideal for stashing away and concealing office clutter. Barrel-shaped African sisal baskets are dyed in many cheerful colors; woven willow baskets from India are tough and sturdy, while round, lacquered Chinese wedding baskets (traditionally used for presenting bridal gifts) stack neatly one on top of each other, so lending themselves perfectly to storage.

Another joy of home workspaces is that the choice of tables and chairs is not dictated by someone else's budget or corporate color scheme. Tables and chairs that reflect one's own tastes make sitting down to work a much more appealing prospect. Old factory or school chairs combined with a retro-style folding picnic table, for example, are a delightfully eclectic and unexpected alternative to typical drab office-style furniture, but make sure they are comfortable if they are to be used for long periods. Alternatively, some modern furniture will marry well with global style and is more likely to be ergonomically designed. The organic lines of Arne Jacobsen's classic "Ant" chair, for example, complements the abstract, ovoid forms of many African carvings—and it looks just as fresh today as it did fifty years ago.

THE WORLD OF WORK *Industrial bins and trolleys left behind by the former owners of this New York warehouse space have been integrated into the design of the advertising agency now in residence (opposite left). In the reception area, the Chinese theme—fortune cookies, lanterns, banners, and newspaper on the floors—works well with a kitsch glass table (opposite right). A London hairdresser's salon has a laidback charm, with the owner combining traditional 1950s barbers' chairs with more global effects, such as custom-made twine-framed mirrors (below) and other exotic finds displayed on a small shelving system (left).*

HOMEWORK *When you only have to please yourself, the workspace at home need follow no conventions or restrictions. A computer is unobtrusively placed within a room of great charm and individuality (above). Only the pile of samples by its side indicate that the owner is a knitwear designer. Wool sits in an African wirework basket and a lively telephone-wire bag dangles from the decorative chair (right). At the other side of London, another designer has allotted a quiet corner to correspondence and general administration (opposite). The "throne" and three-legged stool are African; other artefacts continue the global mood, especially the mask and vellum light.*

GARDENS *It can be only the subtlest of details that add a global element to a garden. Seating offers an opportunity to be adventurous, as this Oriental bench outside an 18th-century house shows (opposite), while exotic statues and treasures can replace traditional pots and urns (below).*

gardens + garden rooms

Outside space can be a stylish extension of the home, providing greenery, fresh air, and a liberating sense of space. Whether you have a tiny city balcony or roof terrace, a shady courtyard or a large backyard, giving your outside space a global flavor will reflect the interior of your home and make it a welcoming environment in which to relax, entertain, or simply enjoy being close to nature. A garden or garden room offers a magical retreat from the stresses of daily life, and should be decorated and furnished with exactly the same interest and care as the other rooms in a home.

Many cultures around the world see the garden as an important and symbolic area of the home. In Morocco, a garden offers an oasis of calm in contrast to the hectic world of the souk, and it also represents the Islamic paradise promised to the faithful by Allah. Designed to please all the senses, Moroccan courtyard gardens are heady with the scents of fruit and flowers and the tranquil sound of running water.

Japanese gardens are also designed as a sanctuary from the complexities of day-to-day life, but the emphasis is on a more refined and rarified air. Instead of rich colors and luxuriant flowers, simple plants and grasses are favored, while areas of swept sand or white pebbles create a serene and spiritual effect. Pebbles or gravel are used to suggest ripples on the surface of still water, while large rounded, standing stones convey stability in a changing world and are thought to represent different moods or spirits. Colorful blooms are eschewed in favor of less ostentatious grasses, which blend with the pebbles or gravel. Fountains are considered distracting, but a flat, calm pond is thought to create a feeling of abundance.

URBAN SPACES *With its fabulous yet functional star-tiled floor, the exotic feel of this inner courtyard belies its northern European setting (opposite). Illusions of hot-country living (right and above) are enhanced by traditional Moroccan pierced metal lanterns that perch on an open dining-room window overlooking a small internal courtyard full of luscious, almost tropical, greenery.*

GARDEN ROOMS *Within a stone's throw of a busy inner-city station, a luxuriant sanctum has been created in what was originally a central stairwell (this page and opposite). Its intimate proportions are given the illusion of greater space due to the clever use of mirrors. The comfortable low-level seating is covered in indigo-dyed fabric from Mali, and an exotic shell collection provides a focal point.*

A good starting point for creating the right mood for a global garden or garden room is the furniture. Wrought iron, rattan or wicker all have a lazy colonial feel, and are reminiscent of sitting on shady verandas cooled by the languidly turning blades of a fan. Wooden garden chairs or loungers can be reupholstered in exotic fabrics, while woven floor mats are ideal for low-level relaxation. Colorful, funky plastic furniture is practical for withstanding summer showers. Thai day beds in templelike red, yellow, and gold make exotic sunloungers. Wooden furniture can be stained dark to create the luxuriant look of hardwood, or bleached to a pale blond tone for a muted oriental effect. For a less formal look, leave furniture exposed to the elements so it can achieve the smooth, sunbleached finish of driftwood.

Plants and flowers are an important part of every garden. For a tropical effect, choose bold plants with glossy jungly leaves or exotic grasses. With plenty of tender loving care, even palms can be grown away from their native tropics, but it is far easier to choose traditional blooms and plant them in a tropical style. Lofty foxgloves and gladioli in fiery hot colors take on a new character when planted amid spears of arid-looking exotic grasses.

For a low-key Japanese look, experiment with the rustling shoots of bamboo. It grows swiftly even in cooler climates, so it is an easy way to create a shelter from wind or simply a veil of privacy from neighbors. In Buddhist countries, the lotus blossom is a symbol of purity as it rises out of the water without being soiled by earth, and water lilies will give a similarly serene touch to a water feature. In planting a garden from scratch, first decide on your predominant colors (for example, tropical shades or muted silvers) and textures (succulent leaves or wispy fronds) and then consult a local garden center for what will work best, given the location and the time available to tend it.

Floors and surfaces add extra texture and interest. Wooden decks have a sporty, casual appeal, while low-maintenance gravel gives a more Japanese flavor. Teamed with clumps of grass or large boulders, it can transform an urban roof garden into somewhere far removed from the hustle and bustle below. Pure white sand is another option for city hideaways. Moorish tiles are a durable surface that provide coolness underfoot during the summer months and are perfect when partnered by a profusion of pot plants in colorful ceramic containers. To conceal uninspiring or dirty brickwork, paint exterior walls pure white or a more adventurous shade. Sugary pastels will conjure up the Caribbean, while more vivid, gaudy hues are reminiscent of Mexico and South America.

CITY SPACES *Even if you live in the heart of an urban development with only a balcony from which to enjoy light and air, don't be inhibited by space restrictions—think fun and funky. Mexico produces some of the brightest and boldest of designs for the most reasonable of prices, like these retro-style chairs (left and opposite right), and plastic flower clothespins that will bring a smile to laundry day (opposite left). For a more sophisticated effect, the owner of this narrow terrace has left an old Thai bench out to be bleached by the sun (below).*

IN AND OUT *Creating an outdoor room is not uncommon in countries that have suitable weather conditions, but presents a challenge in those that haven't! A smart townhouse with a small yard devoid of lawn or flowerbeds (below left) mixes several cultures to achieve a sophisticated global look. Concrete built-in seating is softened by kauna mats from Manipur. The calm minimalist effect is continued with a low-maintenance carpet of gravel. The theme is continued in the first floor roof garden (below right). Where outdoor space is not an option, but indoors there's plenty of room, think creatively. This vast living and working space (opposite) contains a tranquil internal garden with an enormous koi carp pool as its focal point.*

STOCKISTS + SUPPLIERS

The publisher and the author of *Global Style* are not responsible for the products sold by the following companies and it is not our intention to promote any of these purveyors.

Anthropologie
375 West Broadway
New York
NY 10012
212-343-7070
www.anthropologie.com
Clothing, accessories, furniture, and home decor inspired by cultures around the world. Visit their website or call 1-800-309-2500 for details of their stores or to request a catalog.

Authentic Africa
www.authenticafrica.com
An online African art gallery specializing in unique African pieces and tribal art. The objects on offer include hand-crafted tribal and ceremonial dolls and masks, wooden sculptures, and animal skins.

Batavia Interiors
3525 Sacramento Street
San Francisco
CA 94118
415-563-8883
Colonial-style teakwood furniture and decorative accessories imported from Indonesia and India. Also ikat and batik textiles, garden furniture, and vintage pieces.

Chimayo
13029 Ventura Boulevard
Studio City
CA 91604
818-783-0079
www.chimayo@venturablvd.com
Direct importers of an eclectic variety of traditional arts and crafts from Latin America, from unique pieces of folk art, such as Mexican Day of the Dead pieces, to decorative accessories such as ceramics and carvings. Also some pieces from West and Central Africa.

Craft Caravan
63 Greene Street
New York
NY 10012
212-431-6669
Antique global furniture, mostly African in origin, including stools from Ghana and Cameroon, thrones, headrests, baskets, and jewelry from Ethiopia, and textiles and dolls from Togo. Also some furniture from Central Asia.

The Folk Art Gallery
2415 Larkspur Landing Circle
Larkspur
CA 94939
888-276-1553
www.folkartgallery.com
A large selection of handcrafted folk and ethnic art imported from around the world, including items such as African tribal masks, some ceremonial and ritual artifacts, baskets, textiles, jewelry, and ceramics. Many unusual items.

Galerie Renee Antiques
8 East 12th Street
New York
NY 10003
212-929-6870
Global antiques.

Global Village Trading Co.
610-525-2145
email:
info@globalvillagetrading.com
www.globalvillagetrading.com
Agents for contemporary and decorative ethnic arts from Africa, especially Southern Africa. They import unique, colorful, and funky artifacts and traditional African art, including ceramics, wire sculptures, cloth from Mali, and garden sculpture and ornaments. Visit their website to view their stock then phone to place an order.

Indochine
430 Lafayette Street
New York
NY 10027
212-505-5111
Eastern artifacts.

Intérieurs
114 Wooster Street
New York
NY 10012
212-343-0800
Asian-inspired furniture as well as 19th- and 20th-century antiques.

Intermarket
www.indiacraft.com
Antique and modern Indian ethnic furniture for sale on the internet. Armoires, chests, tables, chairs, storage units and accessories.

International Market Gallery
2241 Fillmore Street
San Francisco
CA 94115-2221
415-292-5600
Importers of new and antique tribal rugs, kilim pillows, ethnic and tribal furniture, and cultural artifacts from Korea, Japan, India, Morocco, and Turkey.

Kashmir
157 East 64th Street
New York
NY 10021
212-861-6464
Luxurious Kashmiri goods including textiles and carpets.

Kinnu
43 Spring Street
New York
NY 10012
212-334-4775
Colorful Indian accessories and textiles.

Koan Collection
6109 Melrose Avenue
Los Angeles
CA 90038
213-464-3735
www.koan-collection.com
Colonial furniture, architectural pieces, textiles, tribal artifacts, and jewelry from India, Indonesia, Thailand, and Nepal. Original and modern pieces.

Material Culture
4700 Wissahickon Avenue
Philadelphia
PA 19144
215-849-8030
www.materialculture.com
Beautiful and unique Oriental carpets and Indian and Chinese furniture.

The Nature Source
423 Ridge Road
Queensbury
NY 12804
518-761-6702
www.nature-source.com
*Masks, statues, carvings,
gourds, and other collectibles
from the African continent.*

Orientique
San Francisco Designer
Center
2 Henry Adams Street
Suite 358
San Francisco
CA 94103
415-626-7728
www.orientiqueusa.com
*Chinese antiques and
furniture primarily from the
Ming and Ching dynasties.*

Pier 1 Imports
www.pier1.com
1-800-245-4595
*This chain specializes in
inexpensive and imaginative
merchandise from around the
world. and has 325 stores
across the US. Visit their
website or call the above
number to find the location
of a store in your area.*

Pottery Barn
www.potterybarn.com
1-800-922-5507
*This chain specializes in
attractive, affordable
furniture plus some ethnic-
inspired accessories. Visit
their website or call the above
number to find the location
of a store in your area or to
request a catalog.*

Takashimaya
693 Fifth Avenue
New York, NY 10022
212-350-0100
*Luxurious five-floor New York
branch of the well-known
Japanese department store.*

**Architects and designers
whose work has been
featured in this book**
(numbers following
addresses refer to the pages
on which their work is
featured):

Peter Adler
191 Sussex Gardens
London W2 2RH
+ 44 (0)20 7262 1775
Dealer in original African
and Oceanic tribal art and
craft, pebble jewellery and
rock crystal objects from
India
By appointment only.
*Pages 7 c & far r, 31 tl & tr, 37
r, 43 t, 70–71, 74 l, 83 r, 89,
91 t, 114–115, 129 l, 132–133*

Agnès Emery
Emery & Cie and
Noir d'Ivoire
Rue de l'Hôpital 25–29
Brussels
Belgium
+ 32 (0)2 513 5892
+ 32 (0)2 513 3970 (fax)
*Pages 7 l, 13 r, 22 r, 23, 31 br,
33 r, 38 l, 46 r, 48 r, 50 l, 80
l, 96–97, 112 l, 130–131*

Ellis Flyte
Fashion designer
Fax + 44 (0)20 7431 7560
*Pages 11 l, 21 br, 32, 40 c, 41,
46 l, 66 l, 81 c & r, 102–103,
104–105, 109, 115, 123 r*

Fourth Floor
Hairdressers
4 Northington Street
London WC1N 2JG
*80 r, 90, 124–125, 125 r, 134
r, 134–135*

Intérieurs
114 Wooster Street
New York
NY 10012
USA
+ 1 212 343 0800
Pages 31 bl, 81 l, 84 r

David Mann
MR Architecture + Décor
150 West 28th Street, 1102
New York
NY 10001
USA
+ 1 212 989 9300
+ 1 212 989 9430 (fax)
e-mail ANN@MRARCH.COM
James Corbett can be
contacted through David
Mann.
*Pages 25, 51 c & r, 68 tr,
95 r, 124*

L.A. Morgan
Interior Designer
P. O. Box 39
Hadlyme
CT 06439
USA
+ 1 860 434 0304
+ 1 860 434 3103 (fax)
*Pages 43 b, 50 r, 79, 86–87,
105 r, 107*

Jeff McKay Inc.
**Advertising and Public
Relations Agency**
203 Lafayette Street
New York
NY 10012
USA
+ 1 212 771 1770
*Pages 25, 51 c & r, 68 tr,
95 r, 124*

Paola Piglia
Artist
fax 020 7587 0416
for information and
commissions
*Pages 3, 8, 64–65, 69 l, 92,
117 r, 123 l*

Rebecca & Bryan Purcell
Artists
436 Fort Washington
Avenue
New York
NY 10033
USA
Pages 36 r, 111 l

Michael Reeves
Interiors
33 Mossop Street
London SW3 2NB
+ 44 (0)20 7225 2501
+ 44 (0)20 7225 3060 (fax)
*Pages 10 l, 58 r, 59, 80 c,
136 bl & br*

Johanne Riss
**Stylist, designer and
fashion designer**
35 Place du Nouveau
Marché aux Grains
1000 Brussels
Belgium
+ 32 (0)2 513 0900
+ 32 (0)2 514 3284 (fax)
*Pages 2, 6, 16 l, 53 r, 58 l,
82, 85, 100 r, 113, 136 tr, 137,
140, 144*

Frances Robinson
Detail
**Jewellery designers
and consultants**
+ 44 (0)20 7582 9564
+ 44 (0)20 7587 3783
*Pages 27 r, 44, 67 r, 69 r,
77 l, 118 l, 122*

Marie-France de Saint-Félix
Architect
D.S.F. Creations
52, rue Bichat
Paris 75010
France
+ 33 (0)1 42 39 55 60
+ 33 (0)1 42 45 87 60 (fax)
Pages 24 bl, 36 l, 42, 54 l

Bruno Tanquerel
Artist
2, Passage St. Sébastien
Paris 75011
France
+ 33 (0)1 43 57 03 93
*Pages 22 l, 40 l, 50 c, 91 b,
98–99, 104 l*

Bonnie Young
**Director of global sourcing
and inspiration at Donna
Karan International**
+ 1 212 228 0832
*Pages 10 c, 12 l, 16 r, 36 c,
40 r, 47, 49, 63, 74 c & r, 75,
83 l, 84 l, 106, 119*

PICTURE CREDITS

r = right, l = left, t = top, b = below, c = center

1 spoon from Neal Street East, plate from Selfridges; 2 Johanne Riss' house in Brussels; 3 Paola Piglia's studio in London; 4 gourd from David Wainwright; 6 Johanne Riss' house in Brussels; 7l Agnès Emery's house in Brussels; 7c & far r Peter Adler's house & gallery in London, feather ceremonial hats and white mask from Peter Adler; 8 Paola Piglia's studio in London; 10l Marja Walters – London, designed by Michael Reeves; 10c the brownstone in New York of Bonnie Young, director of global sourcing and inspiration at Donna Karan International; 10r Fourth Floor in London; 11 l Ellis Flyte's house in London; 11r dish from Selfridges; 12l the brownstone in New York of Bonnie Young, director of global sourcing and inspiration at Donna Karan International; 13r Agnès Emery's house in Brussels, bedding from Emery & Cie; 14 wire bowl from David Champion, fabrics from a selection at Neal Street East; 16l Johanne Riss' house in Brussels; 16r the brownstone in New York of Bonnie Young, director of global sourcing and inspiration at Donna Karan International; 16-17 metal bowls from Cane & Able, paperclips from Tribal; 18-19 recycled glass, stone bowl and metal box from David Wainwright, Vietnamese eggshell box from Prue Lane, head of Buddha from V & A Enterprises; 20 & 21tr & bl Etienne & Mary Millner's house in London; 21tl Fourth Floor in London; 21br Ellis Flyte's house in London; 22l an apartment in Paris designed by Bruno Tanquerel; 22r & 23 Agnès Emery's house in Brussels, tiles from Emery & Cie; 24bl La Gelta in Paris designed by Marie-France de Saint-Félix; 25 The Jeff McKay Inc. advertising and public relations agency in New York, designed by David Mann & James Corbett; 26 Indian textiles from Neal Street East; 27r Frances Robinson & Eamonn McMahon's house in London, jewellery from Detail; 28bl Etienne & Mary Millner's house in London, cushions from Missoni at Liberty; 29 shell trimmed fabric from Neal Street East; 31tl & tr Peter Adler's house & gallery in London, fabrics from Peter Adler; 31bl Intérieurs in New York; 31bc silk tablemats from Neal Street East; 31br Agnès Emery's house in Brussels, bedding from Emery & Cie; 32 Ellis Flyte's house in London; 33r Agnès Emery's house in Brussels; 34 bowls from Wing Yip; 36l La Gelta in Paris designed by Marie-France de Saint-Félix; 36c the brownstone in New York of Bonnie Young, director of global

sourcing and inspiration at Donna Karan International; 36r Bryan Purcell, an artist living in New York; 37l Jeff McKay's apartment in New York; 37c Fourth Floor in London; 37r Peter Adler's house & gallery in London, combs and stool from Peter Adler; 38l Agnès Emery's house in Brussels, tiled table from Emery & Cie; 39 Indian ironing board from David Wainwright; 40l an apartment in Paris designed by Bruno Tanquerel; 40c & 41 Ellis Flyte's house in London; 40r the brownstone in New York of Bonnie Young, director of global sourcing and inspiration at Donna Karan International; 42 La Gelta in Paris designed by Marie-France de Saint-Félix; 43t stools from Peter Adler; 43b Kimball Mayer & Meghan Hughes' apartment in New York, designed by L.A. Morgan; 44 Frances Robinson & Eamonn McMahon's house in London, wire dish from Browns; 46l Ellis Flyte's house in London, pottery from Neal Street East; 46r Agnès Emery's house in Brussels; 47 the brownstone in New York of Bonnie Young, director of global sourcing and inspiration at Donna Karan International; 48l Jeff McKay's apartment in New York; 48r Agnès Emery's house in Brussels, lamp from Emery & Cie; 49 the brownstone in New York of Bonnie Young, director of global sourcing and inspiration at Donna Karan International; 50l Agnès Emery's house in Brussels, star light from Emery & Cie; 50c an apartment in Paris designed by Bruno Tanquerel; 50r Kimball Mayer & Meghan Hughes' apartment in New York, designed by L.A. Morgan; 51l lanterns from Old Empire; 51c & r The Jeff McKay Inc. advertising and public relations agency in New York, designed by David Mann & James Corbett; 52 & 52-53 Lassi cup and recycled glass from David Wainwright; 53r Johanne Riss' house in Brussels; 54l La Gelta in Paris designed by Marie-France de Saint-Félix; 54r & 55 Etienne & Mary Millner's house in London, ceramics from Selfridges, chopsticks and small bamboo brush from Neal Street East; 56 Kenyan salad servers and spoon from Tribals, wooden vessels from Old Empire; 57 chopping blocks from David Champion; 58l Johanne Riss' house in Brussels; 58r & 59 Marja Walters - London, designed by Michael Reeves, salt dough plates and bowls from Mint, teapot from Selfridges; 60-61 Lassi glasses from David Wainwright; 62tl spoons from Neal Street East; 62b vase from Nine Schools at Selfridges; 63 the brownstone in New York of Bonnie Young, director of global

sourcing and inspiration at Donna Karan International; 64l soapstone figure from Oxfam; 64r Jeff McKay's apartment in New York; 64-65 Paola Piglia's studio in London; 66l Ellis Flyte's house in London; 67l fetish dolls from David Champion; 67r Frances Robinson & Eamonn McMahon's house in London; 68tr The Jeff McKay Inc. advertising and public relations agency in New York, designed by David Mann & James Corbett; 69l Paola Piglia's studio in London; 69r Frances Robinson & Eamonn McMahon's house in London; 70-71 Peter Adler's house & gallery in London, all items from Peter Adler; 73bcl antique North Indian boots from the Gallery of Antique Costumes & Textiles; 74l bangles from Peter Adler; 74c & r & 75 the brownstone in New York of Bonnie Young, director of global sourcing and inspiration at Donna Karan International; 76r plastic flower from Emma Bernhardt; 77l Frances Robinson & Eamonn McMahon's house in London; 78 Etienne & Mary Millner's house in London; 79 Kimball Mayer & Meghan Hughes' apartment in New York designed by L.A. Morgan; 80l Agnès Emery's house in Brussels; 80c Marja Walters - London, designed by Michael Reeves, matt seating from Ganesha; 80r Fourth Floor in London, sculpture from the Rebecca Hossack Gallery; 81l Intérieurs in New York; 81c & r Ellis Flyte's house in London, tiles from The Life Enhancing Tile Co.; 82 Johanne Riss' house in Brussels; 83l the brownstone in New York of Bonnie Young, director of global sourcing and inspiration at Donna Karan International; 83r Peter Adler's house & gallery in London, cushions from Peter Adler; 84l the brownstone in New York of Bonnie Young, director of global sourcing and inspiration at Donna Karan International; 84r Intérieurs in New York; 85 Johanne Riss' house in Brussels; 86-87 Kimball Mayer & Meghan Hughes' apartment in New York, designed by L.A. Morgan; 88 Karen Harrison's house in London, cushions from Mint; 89 Peter Adler's house & gallery in London, cushion from Peter Adler; 90 Fourth Floor in London, cushions from Ganesha; 91t Peter Adler's house & gallery in London; 91b an apartment in Paris designed by Bruno Tanquerel; 92 Paola Piglia's studio in London, paintings by Paola Piglia; 93 Jeff McKay's apartment in New York; 94 glasses from Urban Outfitters; 95l Chinese honey pot from Wing Yip; 95r The Jeff McKay Inc. advertising and public relations agency in New York, designed by David Mann & James Corbett; 96-97 Agnès Emery's house in Brussels, tiles, star light and African-inspired draw handles from Emery & Cie; 98-99 an apartment in Paris designed by Bruno

Tanquerel; 100r Johanne Riss' house in Brussels; 101 Jeff McKay's apartment in New York; 102-103 Ellis Flyte's house in London; 104l an apartment in Paris designed by Bruno Tanquerel; 104-105 Ellis Flyte's house in London, mug from Neal Street East; 105r Kimball Mayer & Meghan Hughes' apartment in New York designed by L.A. Morgan; 106 the brownstone in New York of Bonnie Young, director of global sourcing and inspiration at Donna Karan International; 107 Kimball Mayer & Meghan Hughes' apartment in New York designed by L.A. Morgan, painting by Erin Parrish; 108 Karen Harrison's house in London; 109 Ellis Flyte's house in London, bedcover from Neal Street East, dresses from Ellis Flyte; 110 antique mirrored bedthrow from the Gallery of Antique Costumes & Textiles, striped throw from Selfridges; 111l Bryan Purcell, an artist living in New York; 111r Etienne & Mary Millner's house in London, Afghanistan patchwork from Liberty; 112l Agnès Emery's house in Brussels, bedlinen and star lamp from Emery & Cie; 112r Jeff McKay's apartment in New York; 113 Johanne Riss' house in Brussels; 114-115 Peter Adler's house & gallery in London; 115 Ellis Flyte's house in London; 116 & 117l Jeff McKay's apartment in New York; 117r Paola Piglia's studio in London; 118l Frances Robinson & Eamonn McMahon's house in London; 118r pyjamas from Abraham & Thakore, head of Buddha from V & A Enterprises; 119 the brownstone in New York of Bonnie Young, director of global sourcing and inspiration at Donna Karan International; 121 cushion from Jaipur, Thai birdcage from Old Empire; 122 Frances Robinson & Eamonn McMahon's house in London; 123l Paola Piglia's studio in London; 123r Ellis Flyte's house in London; 124 The Jeff McKay Inc. advertising and public relations agency in New York, designed by David Mann & James Corbett; 125 Fourth Floor in London; 128 Etienne & Mary Millner's house in London, similar benches from Ormonde Gallery; 129l Peter Adler's house & gallery in London; 130-131 Agnès Emery's house in Brussels, tiles & lanterns from Emery & Cie; 132-133 Peter Adler's house & gallery in London, indigo cloths from Peter Adler; 134-135 Fourth Floor in London, pegs from Emma Bernhardt, chairs from Kitsch 'n' Chic, lantern from Old Empire; 136bl & br Marja Walters - London, designed by Michael Reeves, Kauna mats from Ganesha, bamboo table from Emily Readett Bayley, linen towels from Eastern Trading Allowance; 136tr & 137 Johanne Riss' house in Brussels; 140 Johanne Riss' house in Brussels; 144 Johanne Riss' house in Brussels

INDEX

page numbers in italics refer to captions

A

Africa:
baskets *16–17*, 36, 124
carvings *64*, 92, *118*
decorative techniques *70–71*
dolls and masks *66–67*, 67, *127*
fake flowers *76*
furniture 7, 40, *42–43*, 43, 91, *127*
jewelry 74
kitchenware *56–57*
pottery *14*, 16, 63
stools 7, 40, 43
textiles *26–27*, *31*, 32, 87, *104–105*, *108*, 111, 124, *132*
use of color 16, *16–17*
wirework *14*, *126*
akua ba dolls (from Ghana) 67
altar boxes 69
amulets, lucky 74
"Ant" chair 124
Ashanti people of Ghana 32, 43, 67
azul anul 15, *96*
azulejo ceramics 23

B

babouches 73
bamboo 19, 40, 91, 134
baskets *16–17*, 36, 47, *47*, 92, 124
bathrooms *91*, *114–115*, 115–116
baths *118–119*, 119
batik *30*, 32, *33*, 56, 92, *104–105*, *108–109*, 111, 124
beads/beadwork *71*, 74, *88*
bedlinen *112*
bedrooms/beds 104,
104–105, 106, *106–107*, 107–108, 110, *110–113*
colonial-style 107–108
other furniture 46, *104–105*
bedspreads 28, 32, 108, *108–109*, 110
bookcase screens *86–87*, 123
bracelets/bangles 74, *74*
British East India Company 108
British Raj 47
Buddha *19*, 69, *69*, *118*, 133
buying tips 7, 28, 36, 37
baths/sanitary ware 119
furniture 40
jewelry 74
kitchen/tableware 58, 103

C

cable reel tables 40, *40*
candleholders 51
candlelight 48, *49*, 50–51
ceramics/pottery *6*, 16, 46, *54–55*, 54–58, *58–59*, 103
inspiration from 23
chairs/benches 40, *40–41*, 43, *90*
gardens/garden rooms 128, 133, 134
Joseph Fenby chair *89*
kitchen *29*
workspaces 124, *124–125*
chandeliers *48*
chests 44, 124
China:
furniture 40, *40*, 43, 44, *105*, 107, *111*, *119*, 124
lighting 50, *51*
Ming dynasty 43
porcelain 54–58, *59*
slippers *73*
textiles *31*, 36
use of color 15

chopping blocks *57*
clothing 28, *32–33*
beaded 28, *33*
children's *33*
coffee tables 40, *84*
coir (coconut) mats 16, 25
collections/displays 37, 46, 64, 92, *92*, *120–121*, 122–123, *123*
arrangements/groupings 92, 111, *118*, 119
clothes 28, *32–33*, *109*, *116*, *123*
fake flowers *76–77*
figurative *64–69*, 69
jewelry 74, *74–75*, 92
religious objects *66–69*, *67–69*
shoes *72–73*
color 13
bathrooms *91*, 116, *117*
bedrooms *107*, 108
black and silver *93*
blues 15, *91*, *132*
earthy 16, *16–17*, 32
gardens/garden rooms *132*, 133, 134
greens 15
inspirations for 7, 11, 23
kaleidoscope effect *12–13*
kitchens/eating areas 96–99, *99*
living spaces 84, 87, *90–91*, 91
neutral *18–19*, 19, 84
red 15, *90–91*, 99
vibrant *14–15*, 15
white 19, 84
workspaces 123
yellow 15
concrete 25, 99, *116–117*
garden seating *136*
painted *90*
cooking pots 54, *63*
cooperatives 28
courtyard plantings 23, *130–131*

cupboards/cabinets 44, *44–45*, 99–103
cushions *28–29*, 83, 89, 90, 92
floor cushions *84*, *88*, 91

D

day beds 107, *111*, 133
decking 134, *134–135*
Delft tiles 57
deng/dun chairs 43
Dia de los Muertos (Mexican Day of the Dead) mementoes 69, *123*
display cabinets 44
distemper 25

F

fair trade 7, 28
fetish dolls 67, *67*
floor lights 87
floors/flooring 16, 19, *22–24*, 25
defining areas *86–87*, 123
gardens/garden rooms *131*, 134
informal finishes *24*, 25, *25*
kitchens/eating areas 99, 103
flowers/plants 83, *90*, 92, 130, *130*, 133–134
fake *76–77*
focal points 37
funerary posts *67–69*
furniture 7, 37, *38–39*, 39, 91
decorating 47
garden/garden rooms *128*, *132*, 133
kitchens/eating areas 96
workspaces *123*, 124, *124–125*
see also bedrooms/beds; living spaces *and specific types*

G

gardens + garden rooms *128–136*, *129–130*, *133–134*
city spaces *134–135*
sleeping in 111
glassware 7, 36, *52–53*, 54
see also lighting; mirrors
global style:
choosing pieces 36, 39
defined 7, 36
see also buying tips
good luck hangings *14*, 15, 28
gourds 63
grave markers 69
guest bedrooms *108–109*

H

hammocks 111
hanbel 32
hansi 74
hip baths 119
home offices *see* workspaces
hutches *46*, 103

I

India:
furniture 47, 91, 107–108, *118*, 124
jewelry 74
kitchenware 54, 63, 103
metalwork *16–17*, 36, *52–53*, *98–99*
slippers *73*
textiles *26*, 28, *29*, 32, 87, *123*
mirror embroidery *14*, *26*, 28, *110*
saris *27*, 28
use of color 11, 15
Iznik ceramics 23

J

Japan:
ceramics 57–58

colors 19
furniture 40, 44, 124
gardens 130
interiors 91
textiles 7
kimonos *31*, *32*, *84*
lacquerwork 44
jootis 73
jute matting 25

K

katab cloth 28
Kente cloth *31*, *32*
kilims 19, *29*, 32, *108–109*
    wall-hung 27, *28*, 87
kitchens + eating areas
    94–95, 95, *96–97*,
    96–102, *98–99*, *102–103*
kitchenware + tableware
    37, *52–54*, 53, *54–57*,
    60–63, 63, *94*, *100–101*,
    103
    wooden items *56–57*,
    62–63, 63
kneading bowl 63
Kuba cloth 32
Kuba people of Zaire 32, *69*

L

lacquerwork 44
    imitation 40
lamps + lighting 48, *48–51*,
    50–51, *127*
    bedroom 111
    gardens *130*
    kitchens/eating areas
    96, 103
    living spaces 87
lampshades 50, *50*, 87, *95*
lanterns 50–51, *50–51*, 87
Liberty print *33*
living spaces 83, *84–87*,
    86–87, 91, *137*
    details 92, *92–93*
    low-level *84–85*, 91
love dolls *104*
lucky charms 74

M

mandi 116
marriage chest 44

Masai tribe *69*
masks, tribal/ceremonial *66*,
    67
mats/matting 16, *24*, 25, *85*
metalwork *16–17*, 36,
    52–53, *60–61*, *112*
Meissen pottery 57
Mexico:
    fake flowers *76*
    furniture *107–108*, *134–135*
    glassware 7, 36, *52–53*, 54
    ponchos and blankets
    14–15
    religious objects *66*, 69
    tiles 23
mirrors 45, *116*, *125*, *132*
Morocco:
    furniture *38*, 108
    gardens 130
    kitchen/tableware *54*, 103
    lighting 50, 51, *96*
    slippers *73*
    textiles *31*, *32*, *112*
mud cloth 32

N

newspaper as floorcovering
    25, *124*
nkonnua fufuo/tuntum 43

O

occasional tables *38–39*
ostrich eggs 63
Ottoman empire 108

P

paraths 63
patchwork, Victorian *28–29*
pattern and motifs
    16, *16–17*, 27, *28–31*
    Islamic *22*, 23, 32, 44
pestles and mortars 63
pisé mud 16, 23

R

raffia cloth 16, 32
raku (Japanese stoneware)
    57
reclamation/recycling
    40, *52–53*, *60–61*, 95,
    120, 124

retablos 69
rice 63
rice bowls 58
rice spoons 63
rugs 19, *31*, 32, *86–87*
    flat woven *see* kilims

S

saddlebags 32
salvaged objects 7, 40, *40*,
    119
scholar's desk, Chinese *86*
screens/screening *86–87*,
    91, 95, 103, 123
sculpture 19
seagrass matting 16
seating 44
    low-level *132*
    see also chairs/benches
Shaka Zulu 74
shell decoration 26, 28, *29*,
    70, 88
shodana (Japanese display
    cabinet) 44
showers/showering *23*, 116,
    119
shrines *68*, 69
side tables 40, 43, *43*, 92,
    105
Silk Route 32
silks 7, 32, 36, 87
    tie-dyed *14*
simplicity/minimalism
    38–39, 39, *58–59*, *115*,
    136
    bathrooms *114–115*
    bedrooms *106–107*, 108
    gardens *136*
    living spaces 83, *84–87*,
    84–87, 91
singing bowls *63*
soapstone figures (African)
    64–65, 92
sofas/divans 91, *91*, 108
souvenirs 7, *17*, *30*, *56*, *73*,
    122–3, 123
spoons and ladles *62*, 63
spotlights 87
stainless steel 99, *101*
stools 7, 40, *42–43*, 43
storage 44, *44–45*, 47, *47*

kitchens 99, *99–103*, *103*
    workspaces 120, *122–123*,
    123–124, *124*, *126*
surface + texture *10–11*, 20,
    20–21, *22–23*, *23–25*,
    24, *25*
    bathrooms 116, *116–117*
    contrasting *18–19*
    gardens/garden rooms
    130, 134
    kitchens/eating areas 96,
    98–99, 99
    living spaces 87
swinging beds 107

T

table coverings 28
tableaux, religious *68*
tables *38–39*, 40, *40*
    low-level *84–85*, 91
    side 40, 43
    workspaces *123*, 124, *124*
tableware *see* kitchenware +
    tableware
tansu (Japanese storage
    chest) 44
tatami matting 11, 25
teahouses 91
teapots 53, 58, *59*
textiles 7, *14–15*, 16, *17*,
    26–27, 27, 28, *28–33*,
    32, 87
    inspiration from 11
    *see also under country and
    specific types*
texture *see* surface + texture
Thar desert, India 23
"Thrones" (African seating)
    40, *123*, *126*
Tibetan singing bowls *62*
tiles *22–23*, 23, 57
    bathrooms *115*, *116–19*
    gardens/garden rooms
    131, 134
    kitchens/eating areas 96,
    96–97, 99
tokonoma (recess
    in Japanese teahouses)
    108
toran cloths *14*, 15, 28
Tribeca loft living *86–87*, 107

"Turkish rooms" 40
tutini (Aboriginal grave
    markers) 69

V

vellum lights 48, 50
votive figures *64–65*

W

wall finishes 16, 19, *21*,
    23–25, *24*, 90, *116–117*
    gardens/garden rooms
    132, 134
wall hangings 27, 28, *28*, *31*,
    32
wall lights 87
Warenga people of Zaire 69
wedding baskets 124
Wedgwood pottery 57
"white stools" 43
whitewash 11, 25
willow-pattern dishes 57
window treatments 28
wood
    ebony 40
    mahogany 40
workspaces 120, *120–121*,
    122–123, *123–124*,
    124–125, *126–127*, *137*
worksurfaces *98*, 99

Z

zillij 23
zulus 74

ACKNOWLEDGMENTS

Many many thanks to Catherine for rising to the challenge so spectacularly and producing these inspiring photographs. Thanks to Hannah Terrett, friend, assistant, and very special individual. To Jo Leevers, admiration and thanks for her incredible efficiency and talent. Penny Tattersall deserves a big thank you from Catherine and I for being the loveliest agent in the business and supporting us all the way.

A huge thank you goes to all the people, friends, and strangers, who let us into their amazing homes and workspaces with such good grace. I'm indebted to the team at Ryland Peters & Small for the chance to produce this book and for all the hard work they have put into it.

I would like to say a special thank you to my Mum and Dad who were with me in mind and spirit while facing their own challenges, and all my family and friends for their enthusiasm.

Finally, to Letty, my daughter, a gigantic kiss and cuddle for being so involved and joining in the big adventure!